EDITED BY LISA PURCELL

CLASSIC
CIVIL WAR STORIES

TWENTY EXTRAORDINARY
TALES OF THE NORTH AND SOUTH

MJF BOOKS
NEW YORK

Published by MJF Books
Fine Communications
322 Eighth Avenue
New York, NY 10001

Classic Civil War Stories
LC Control Number 2007920104
ISBN-13: 978-1-56731-860-9
ISBN-10: 1-56731-860-6

QM   10   9   8   7   6   5   4   3   2   1

To Johnathan
Between every passion is beer.

Contents

Introduction

War is cruelty. There is no use trying
to reform it. The crueler it is,
the sooner it will be over.

—*General William T. Sherman*

As no other war, the Civil War has captured the American imagination. This is not surprising: It had great leaders, such as Abraham Lincoln, Robert E. Lee, Ulysses S. Grant, Stonewall Jackson, and William T. Sherman. It had great battles, too, such as Shiloh, Chickamauga, Antietam, and Gettysburg. This war—the only war fought on American soil, between Americans—was surely one of the most heroic and the most horrific. During the four years of this brutal, bloody conflict, Americans killed each other in greater numbers than in any war before or since. The Civil War left the

Southern Confederacy defeated and the Union intact, and it ended slavery, all at the cost of nearly 1,100,000 casualties and more than 620,000 lives.

Between the first shots fired at Fort Sumter on April 12, 1861, to Lee's surrender to Grant at Appomattox on April 9, 1865, the nation was irrevocably changed. Homes were transformed into headquarters; churches and schools into makeshift hospitals. Marauding armies decimated the once-peaceful landscape, pillaging farms, burning towns, and killing each other wherever they met. And whether soldier or civilian, the lives of those who lived through the war were irrevocably changed, too.

This collection of stories examines a few of those lives, focusing on personal experiences of the war. How did it feel to be a soldier in the field, facing enemy fire while friends dropped beside you? In the conflict known as the "Brothers' War," how did one live with the decision to take up arms against a neighbor, a brother, a father? What was life like for the widow trying to protect her plantation while Sherman's troops rampaged across her land? Could a Northern captain fall in love with his Southern enemy? Some of the stories included here are factual, others are fiction. Some were published before the war had ended and others more than half a century later, but all bring to life the experience of the common person coping with a devastating conflict.

Both the North and the South entered into the war with high hopes and high spirits, each side sure that they would quickly defeat the other and bring about a quick end to hostilities. In the early days, the war was a spectacle, with the soldiers as its stars. Missouri–born novelist Winston Churchill's "Camp Jackson" offers us a glimpse of this spectacle. As regiments begin to assemble on Secession Monday in St. Louis, citizens are filled with a giddy sense of adventure, especially the swooning young women who imagine their heroes' upcoming victories for the South. Many Southerners, however, did not find choosing sides to be as easy a matter as did those ardent young women. John Fox, Jr., illustrates the dilemma many faced in "The Blue or the Gray," when a young Kentuckian must question everything he grew up believing in order to make his own hard decision.

Divided loyalties is a recurring theme in Civil War fiction. Stephen Crane, who wrote one of the most famous Civil War novels, *The Red Badge of Courage*, offers his version in "A Grey Sleeve." Here, a feisty young Southern woman steps up against a Northern captain in order to protect her home and family— and enchants her would-be enemy in the process. Both of them must then face the consequences of a nation divided.

Newspaper columnist, satirist, essayist, short-story writer, and novelist Ambrose Bierce also chose to illustrate the consequences of divided loyalties in the haunting short story, "A Horseman in the Sky." Bierce was himself a veteran of the war, fighting for the Union at several major battles, including Shiloh and Chickamauga, before he was severely wounded in the head at Kennesaw Mountain. "A Horseman in the Sky" is the tale of Carter Druse, a young Virginian whose conscience tells him he must fight for the Union. This is a heartbreaking decision for his proud Southern father, who can only tell him, "Well, go, sir, and whatever may occur do what you conceive to be your duty. . . ." For this one young man, however, following that advice costs him that which is most precious to him.

By the late 1800s and early 1900s, with the war a respectable distance in the past, it had become easy to romanticize soldiers' lives—especially those of the South. Joseph A. Altsheler was one of many turn-of-the-century authors who set his tales in the midst of the war. Altsheler, a prolific writer, turned out several novels featuring a company of Southern soldiers, the "Invincibles," who in the selection here from *The Guns of Bull Run* face the first decisive battle of the war. But war is not all exciting battles—it has even been described as "long periods of boredom, punctuated by moments of pure terror." While many of the selections in this book deal with those moments of terror, "The Tedium of Camp" is a rare piece that focuses on one of the long periods of boredom. After many days of filling those endless hours, the young hero of this fictional account by John McElroy must choose between taking a position as hospital steward to the company's surgeon—which will keep him out of harm's way—or sticking it out and fighting side by side with his fellow soldiers.

Fascination with the Civil War was not restricted to Americans; "A Prisoner" comes from English novelist G. A. Henty, who wrote adventure stories for boys. Another prolific writer, Henty was known for his careful research and attention to historical detail. Tackling subjects as diverse as the fall of Jerusalem to the Napoleonic wars, he found that the American Civil War offered him as much drama as any Old World conflict.

In contrast to the romanticism of most turn-of-the-century writers, the work of Ambrose Bierce is far more realistic, whether he was writing short stories or nonfiction pieces. Bierce wrote gritty, often disturbing tales of wartime experience. His "What I Saw of Shiloh" is an idiosyncratic account of this famous battle, which in two days claimed a greater number of American lives than all previous wars combined.

While the general citizenry of the South faced the terrors of the war on a daily basis, comparatively few battles were waged north of the Mason-Dixon line. One exception, and one of the most famous battles in American history, took place in Gettysburg, Pennsylvania. The account of that battle included here, "The Fourteenth at Gettysburg," first appeared in *Harper's Weekly* in 1863.

There seem to be few subjects about which Mark Twain did not take up pen, and the Civil War was no exception. In his classic *Life on the Mississippi,* as he steams past Vicksburg, Mississippi—well known for its famous caves—he recounts the story of a couple who lived through the city's shelling between May and July of 1863. Another account of these trying days, first published in 1864, is Mary Ann Loughborough's *My Cave Life in Vicksburg,* a vivid chronicle of the terror and uncertainty of life in a city under bombardment.

The battlefield combatants were men (with a few exceptions), but women were no less affected by the war. Many women volunteered as nurses, cooks, and even spies. In 1863 Louisa May Alcott, most famous for *Little Women,* published *Hospital Sketches,* which chronicles her wartime experiences as a nurse in Washington, D.C. Although written with humor and a light touch, there is no disguising the pain of trying to save the lives of the shattered young soldiers who poured regularly into the wards, or of watching helplessly as one of them dies. Alcott's stint as a nurse was brief—only six weeks. While on duty, Alcott contracted typhoid pneumonia, from which she nearly died and never fully recovered; nurses were no less susceptible to the diseases that swept through hospital wards than were the patients. The chances of a wounded soldier surviving, even after treatment, were slight. "A Night Ride of the Wounded" from Randall Parrish vividly captures the trauma of being transported from the battlefield to one of the makeshift hospitals, where facilities were primitive at best, medical treatments still crude, and conditions unsanitary.

Like Alcott, many Northern and Southern women volunteered for duty in army hospitals as a way to serve their cause. Often inexperienced, many times from pampered backgrounds, they nonetheless rose to the challenge of this backbreaking—and heartbreaking—work. Phoebe Yates Levy Pember was a well-educated woman from a prosperous Jewish family in Charleston, South Carolina. A widow by 1861, she accepted the offer to serve as matron at the largest military hospital in the country at that time, Chimborazo Hospital in Richmond, Virginia. Even in this large and established facility, casualties were greatly compounded by severe shortages of personnel, food, medicine, and equipment. As did Alcott, Pember began her service in December 1862, but her stint lasted far longer. She remained at Chimborazo even after the fall of Richmond, until Union troops took it over. During that time, she did whatever she could to relieve her patients' miseries— from playing cards with recovering patients to holding the hands of dying young men. During her time at Chimborazo, she noticed the regard her Southern boys felt for their Northern counterparts. Yet, as the suffering in the South intensified, so did the hatred toward the foe. "Intensification of Suffering and Hatred" is an excerpt from Pember's *A Southern Woman's Story,* which takes place in 1864 as the war was grinding to a close.

It is true of many wars that combatants hold their enemies in high regard. A fictional account of the esteem that Northerners and Southerners could feel for each other even in the thick of battle comes from turn-of-the-century novelist George Washington Cable. Richard Thorndyke Smith, a nineteen-year-old soldier from New Orleans, seems almost to hero-worship one particular Yankee enemy, Captain Jewett, the "most daring Union scout between Vicksburg and New Orleans." In this excerpt, "The Charge in the Lane" from *The Cavalier,* Dick must help the mortally wounded Jewett get off the battlefield.

For women who wanted to get close to the battlefield, there were few options other than nursing or cooking. One woman, however, S. Emma E. Edmonds, first adopted the identity of "Franklin Thompson" in order to enlist in a Michigan volunteer infantry company. Her disguise was successful, and she participated in several battles, including First Bull Run, the Peninsular Campaign, Antietam, and Fredericksburg. She also relied on her successful ability to transform herself—usually into an Irish woman or a black man—to serve as a spy for the troops. In the excerpt included here from *Nurse and Spy in the Union Army,* she describes donning one of her disguises to penetrate enemy lines.

Women such as Alcott, Pember, and Edmonds chose to work in the thick of things, but staying at home was no guarantee of security for women, especially those of the South. With so many men away fighting the war, women were left on their own to run businesses, farms, and entire plantations without help from their husbands, fathers, or sons. Dolly Sumner Lunt, a widow who kept a plantation in Georgia with her small daughter, Sadai, and what was left of her slaves, details the terrifying days of Sherman's march to the sea that took the army through her hometown and her home.

From middle-aged widows defending their homes to young men entering into their first skirmishes, war changes the lives of everyone it touches and brings out qualities that they never knew they possessed, from bravery to cowardice and every shade in between. Sometimes it brings out a sheer tenacity not to fall without giving every ounce of your being to the fight. A stirring entry, "The Last Shot," by Violetta, describes the almost mindless determination of a Northern gunner to take down his enemy before he himself falls.

Soldiers valued the comrades who stood beside them through the horrific battles of the war. They also valued the artillery they had dragged through thousands of miles of mud and blood over four long years. In an oddly poignant entry from Thomas Nelson Page, "The Burial of the Guns," we read about the history of a few trusted guns carried by one Southern company and the men's final tribute to them when they are told to lay down their weapons after Lee's surrender.

The last selection expresses the uncertainty of life after the war was finally declared over. Weapons may have been lowered and men wearily returned home, but would the nation heal from its wounds and reunite? Dolly Sumner Lunt in her journal entry of April 29, 1865, asks a question that may still not be fully answered: "Where are we now?"

Classic

CIVIL WAR STORIES

Camp Jackson

[**WINSTON CHURCHILL**]

What enthusiasm on that gusty Monday morning, the Sixth of May, 1861! Twelfth Street to the north of the Market House is full three hundred feet across, and the militia of the Sovereign State of Missouri is gathering there. Thence by order of her Governor they are to march to Camp Jackson for a week of drill and instruction.

Half a mile nearer the river, on the house of the Minute Men, the strange flag leaps wildly in the wind this day.

On Twelfth Street the sun is shining, drums are beating, and bands are playing, and bright aides dashing hither and thither on spirited chargers. One by one the companies are marching up, and taking place in line; the city companies in natty gray fatigue, the country companies often in their Sunday clothes. But they walk with heads erect and chests out, and the ladies wave their gay parasols and cheer them. Here are the aristocratic St. Louis Grays, Company A; there come the Washington Guards and Washington Blues, and Laclede Guards and Missouri Guards and Davis Guards. Yes, this is Secession Day, this Monday. And the colors are the Stars and Stripes and the Arms of Missouri crossed.

What are they waiting for? Why don't they move? Hark! A clatter and a cloud of dust by the market place, an ecstasy of cheers running in waves the length of the crowd. Make way for the dragoons! Here they come at last, four and four, the horses prancing and dancing and pointing quivering ears at the tossing sea of hats and parasols and ribbons. Maude Catherwood squeezes Virginia's arm. There, riding in front, erect and firm in the saddle, is Captain Clarence Colfax. Virginia is red and white, and red again,—true colors of the Confederacy. How proud she was of him now! How ashamed that she even doubted him! Oh, that was his true calling, a soldier's life. In that moment she saw him at the head of armies, from the South, driving the Yankee hordes northward and still northward until the roar of the lakes warns them of annihilation. She saw his chivalry sparing them. Yes, this is Secession Monday.

Down to a trot they slow, Clarence's black thoroughbred arching his long neck, proud as his master of the squadron which follows, four and four. The square young man of bone and sinew in the first four, whose horse is built like a Crusader's, is George Catherwood. And Eugenie gives a cry and points to the rear where Maurice is riding.

Whose will be the Arsenal now? Can the Yankee regiments with their slouchy Dutchmen hope to capture it! If there are any Yankees in Twelfth Street that day, they are silent. Yes, there are some. And there are some, even in the ranks of this Militia— who will fight for the Union. These are sad indeed.

There is another wait, the companies standing at ease. Some of the dragoons dismount, but not the handsome young captain, who rides straight to the bright group which has caught his eye, Colonel Carvel wrings his gauntleted hand.

"Clarence, we are proud of you, sir," he says.

And Virginia, repeats his words, her eyes sparkling, her fingers caressing the silken curve of Jefferson's neck.

"Clarence, you will drive Captain Lyon and his Hessians into the river."

"Hush, Jinny," he answered, "we are merely going into camp to learn to drill, that we may be ready to defend the state when the time comes."

Virginia laughed. "I had forgotten," she said.

"You will have your cousin court-martialed, my dear," said the Colonel.

Just then the call is sounded. But he must needs press Virginia's hand first, and allow admiring Maude and Eugenie to press his. Then he goes off at a slow canter to join his dragoons, waving his glove at them, and turning to give the sharp order, "Attention!" to his squadron.

Virginia is deliriously happy. Once more she has swept from her heart every vestige of doubt. Now is Clarence the man she can admire. Chosen unanimously captain of the Squadron but a few days since, Clarence had taken command like a veteran. George Catherwood and Maurice had told the story.

And now at last the city is to shake off the dust of the North. "On to Camp Jackson!" was the cry. The bands are started, the general and staff begin to move, and the column swings into the Olive Street road, followed by a concourse of citizens awheel and afoot, the horse cars crowded. Virginia and Maude and the Colonel in the Carvel carriage, and behind Ned, on the box, is their luncheon in a hamper. Standing up, the girls can just see the nodding plumes of the dragoons far to the front. . . .

Into Lindell Grove flocked the crowd, the rich and the poor, the proprietor and the salesmen, to watch the soldiers pitch their tents under the spreading trees. The gallant dragoons were off to the west, across a little stream which trickled through the grounds. By the side of it Virginia and Maude, enchanted, beheld Captain Colfax shouting his orders while his troopers dragged the canvas from the wagons, and staggered under it to the line. Alas! That the girls were there! The Captain lost his temper, his troopers, perspiring over Gordian knots in the ropes, uttered strange soldier oaths, while the mad wind which blew that day played a hundred pranks.

To the discomfiture of the young ladies, Colonel Carvel pulled his goatee and guffawed. Virginia was for moving away.

"How mean, Pa," she said indignantly. "How can you expect them to do it right the first day, and in this wind?"

"Oh! Jinny, look at Maurice!" exclaimed Maude, giggling. "He is pulled over on his head."

The Colonel roared. And the gentlemen and ladies who were standing by laughed, too. Virginia did not laugh. It was all too serious for her.

"You will see that they can fight," she said. "They can beat the Yankees and Dutch."

This speech made the Colonel glance around him: Then he smiled,—in response to other smiles.

"My dear," he said, "you must remember that this is a peaceable camp of instruction of the state militia. There fly the Stars and Stripes from the general's tent. Do you see that they are above the state flag? Jinny; you forget yourself."

Jinny stamped her foot

"Oh, I hate dissimulation," she cried. "Why can't we say outright that we are going to run that detestable Captain Lyon and his Yankees and Hessians out of the Arsenal?"

"Why not, Colonel Carvel?" cried Maude. She had forgotten that one of her brothers was with the Yankees and Hessians.

"Why aren't women made generals and governors?" said the Colonel.

"If we were," answered Virginia, "something might be accomplished."

"Isn't Clarence enough of a fire-eater to suit you?" asked her father.

But the tents were pitched, and at that moment the young Captain was seen to hand over his horse to an orderly, and to come toward them. He was followed by George Catherwood.

"Come, Jinny," cried her cousin, "let us go over to the main camp."

"And walk on Davis Avenue," said Virginia, flushing with pride. "Isn't there a Davis Avenue?"

"Yes, and a Lee Avenue, and a Beauregard Avenue," said George, taking his sister's arm.

"We shall walk in them all," said Virginia.

What a scene of animation it was. The rustling trees and the young grass of early May, and the two hundred and forty tents in lines of military precision. Up and down the grassy streets flowed the promenade, proud fathers and mothers, and sweethearts and sisters and wives in gala dress. Wear your bright gowns now, you devoted women. The day is coming when you will make them over and over again, or tear them to lint, to stanch the blood of these young men who wear their new gray so well.

Every afternoon Virginia drove with her father and her aunt to Camp Jackson. All the fashion and beauty of the city were there. The bands played, the black coachmen flecked the backs of their shining horses, and walking in the avenues or seated under the trees were natty young gentlemen in white trousers and brass buttoned jackets. All was not soldier fare at the regimental messes. Cakes and jellies and even ices and more substantial dainties were laid beneath those tents. Dress parade was one long sigh of delight: Better not to have been born than to been a young man in St. Louis, early in Camp Jackson week, and not be a militiaman.

The Blue or the Gray

[JOHN FOX, JR.]

In the far North, as in the far South, men had but
to drift with the tide. Among the Kentuckians,
the forces that moulded her sons—Davis and
Lincoln—were at war in the State, as they were at
war in the nation. By ties of blood, sympathies, insti-
tutions, Kentucky was bound fast to the South. Yet,
ten years before, Kentuckians had demanded the
gradual emancipation of the slave. That far back,
they had carved a pledge on a block of Kentucky
marble, which should be placed in the Washington
monument, that Kentucky would be the last to give
up the Union. For ten years, they had felt the
shadow of the war creeping toward them. In the
dark hours of that dismal year, before the dawn of
final decision, the men, women, and children of
Kentucky talked of little else save war, and the skeleton of war took its place in the closet or every home

from the Ohio to the crest of the Cumberland. When the dawn of that decision came, Kentucky spread before the world a record of independent-mindedness, patriotism, as each side saw the word, and sacrifice that has no parallel in history. She sent the flower of her youth—forty thousand strong—into the Confederacy; she lifted the lid of her treasury to Lincoln, and in answer to his every call, sent him a soldier, practically without a bounty and without a draft. And when the curtain fell on the last act of the great tragedy, half of her manhood was behind it—helpless from disease, wounded, or dead on the battlefield.

So, on a gentle April day, when the great news came, it came like a sword that, with one stroke, slashed the State in twain, shearing through the strongest bonds that link one man to another, whether of blood, business, politics or religion, as though they were no more than threads of wool. Nowhere in the Union was the National drama so played to the bitter end in the confines of a single State. As the nation was rent apart, so was the commonwealth; as the State, so was the county; as the county, the neighborhood; as the neighborhood, the family; and as the family, so brother and brother, father and son. In the nation the kinship was racial only. Brother knew not the face of brother. There was distance between them, antagonism, prejudice, a smouldering dislike easily fanned to flaming hatred.

In Kentucky the brothers had been born in the same
bed, slept in the same cradle, played under the same
roof, sat side by side in the same schoolroom, and
stood now on the threshold of manhood arm in
arm, with mutual interests, mutual love, mutual
pride in family that made clan feeling peculiarly
intense. For antislavery fanaticism, or honest unionism, one needed not to go to the far North; as, for
imperious, hotheaded, non-interference or pure State
sovereignty, one needed not to go to the far South.
They were all there in the State, the county, the family—under the same roof. Along the border alone
did feeling approach uniformity—the border of
Kentucky hills. There unionism was free from prejudice as nowhere else on the continent save elsewhere throughout the Southern mountains. Those
Southern Yankees knew nothing about the valley
aristocrat, nothing about his slaves, and cared as little
for one as for the other. Since '76 they had known
but one flag, and one flag only, and to that flag
instinctively they rallied. But that the State should
be swept from border to border with horror, there
was division even here: for, in the Kentucky mountains, there was, here and there, a patriarch like Joel
Turner who owned slaves, and he and his sons
fought for them as he and his sons would have
fought for their horses, or their cattle, or their sheep.

It was the prescient horror of such a condition that
had no little part in the neutral stand that Kentucky

strove to maintain. She knew what war was—for every fireside was rich in memories that men and women had of kindred who had fallen on numberless battlefields—back even to St. Clair's defeat and the Raisin massacre; and though she did not fear war for its harvest of dangers and death, she did look with terror on a conflict between neighbors, friends, and brothers. So she refused troops to Lincoln; she refused them to Davis. Both pledged her immunity from invasion, and, to enforce that pledge, she raised Home Guards as she had already raised State Guards for internal protection and peace. And there—as a State—she stood: but the tragedy went on in the Kentucky home—a tragedy of peculiar intensity and pathos in one Kentucky home—the Deans'.

Harry had grown up tall, pale, studious, brooding. He had always been the pet of his Uncle Brutus— the old Lion of White Hall. Visiting the Hall, he had drunk in the poison, or consecration, as was the point of view, of abolitionism. At the first sign he was never allowed to go again. But the poison had gone deep. Whenever he could he went to hear old Brutus speak. Eagerly he heard stories of the fearless abolitionist's hand-to-hand fights with men who sought to skewer his fiery tongue. Deeply he brooded on every word that his retentive ear had caught from the old man's lips, and on the wrongs he endured in behalf of his cause and for freedom of speech.

One other hero did he place above him—the great commoner after whom he had been christened, Henry Clay Dean. He knew how Clay's life had been devoted to averting the coming war, and how his last days had been darkly shadowed by the belief that, when he was gone, the war must come. At times he could hear that clarion voice as it rang through the Senate with the bold challenge to his own people that paramount was his duty to the nation—subordinate his duty to his State. Who can tell what the nation owed, in Kentucky, at least, to the passionate allegiance that was broadcast through the State to Henry Clay? It was not in the boy's blood to be driven an inch, and no one tried to drive him. In his own home he was a spectre of gnawing anguish to his mother and Margaret, of unspeakable bitterness and disappointment to his father, and an impenetrable sphinx to Dan. For in Dan there was no shaking doubt. He was the spirit, incarnate, of the young, unquestioning, unthinking, generous, reckless, hotheaded, passionate South.

And Chad? The news reached Major Buford's farm at noon, and Chad went to the woods and came in at dusk, haggard and spent. Miserably now he held his tongue and tortured his brain. Purposely, he never opened his lips to Harry Dean. He tried to make known to the Major the struggle going on within him, but the iron-willed old man brushed away all argument with an impatient wave of his hand. With Margaret he talked once, and straightway the question was dropped like a living coal. So, Chad withdrew from his fellows. The social life of the town, gayer than ever now, knew him no more. He kept up his college work, but when he was not at his books, he walked the fields, and many a moonlit midnight found him striding along a white turnpike, or sitting motionless on top of a fence along the border of some woodland, his chin in both hands, fighting his fight out in the cool stillness alone. He himself little knew the unmeant significance there was in the old Continental uniform he had worn to the dance. Even his old rifle, had he but known it, had been carried with Daniel Morgan from Virginia to Washington's aid in Cambridge. His earliest memories of war were rooted in thrilling stories of King's Mountain. He had heard old men tell of pointing deadly rifles at red-coats at New Orleans, and had absorbed their own love of Old Hickory. The schoolmaster himself, when a mere lad, had been with Scott in Mexico. The spirit of the backwoodsman had been caught in the hills, and was alive and unchanged at that very hour. The boy was practically born in Revolutionary days, and that was why, like all mountaineers, Chad had little love of State and only love of country—was first, last and all the time, simply American. It was not reason—it was instinct. The heroes the schoolmaster had taught him to love and some day to emulate, had fought under one flag, and, like them, the mountaineers never dreamed there could be another. And so the boy was an unconscious reincarnation of that old spirit, uninfluenced by temporary apostasies in the outside world, untouched absolutely by sectional prejudice or the appeal of the slave. The mountaineer had no hatred of the valley aristocrat, because he knew nothing of him, and envied no man what he was, what he had, or the life he led. So, as for slavery, that question, singularly enough, never troubled his soul. To him slaves were hewers of wood and drawers of water. The Lord had made them so, and the Bible said that it was right. That the school-master had taught Chad. He had read "Uncle Tom's Cabin," and the story made him smile. The tragedies of it he had never known and he did not believe. Slaves were sleek, well-fed, well-housed, loved and trusted, rightly inferior and happy; and no aristocrat ever moved among them with a more lordly, right-eous air of authority than did this mountain lad who had known them little more than half a dozen years. Unlike the North, the boy had no prejudice, no antagonism, no jealousy, no grievance to help him in his struggle. Unlike Harry, he had no slave sympa-thy to stir him to the depths, no stubborn, rebellious pride to prod him on. In the days when the school-master thundered at him some speech of the Prince of Kentuckians, it was always the national thrill in the fiery utterance that had shaken him even then.

So that unconsciously the boy was the embodiment of pure Americanism, and for that reason he and the people among whom he was born stood among the millions on either side, quite alone.

What was he fighting then—ah, what? If the bedrock of his character was not loyalty, it was nothing. In the mountains the Turners had taken him from the Wilderness. In the Bluegrass the old Major had taken him from the hills. His very life he owed to the simple, kindly mountaineers, and what he valued more than his life he owed to the simple gentleman who had picked him up from the roadside and, almost without question, had taken him to his heart and to his home. The Turners, he knew, would fight for their slaves as they would have fought Dillon or Devil had either proposed to take from them a cow, a hog, or a sheep. For that Chad could not blame them. And the Major was going to fight, as he believed, for his liberty, his State, his country, his property, his fireside. So in the eyes of both, Chad must be the snake who had warmed his frozen body on their hearthstones and bitten the kindly hands that had warmed him back to life. What would Melissa say? Mentally he shrank from the fire of her eyes and the scorn of her tongue when she should know. And Margaret—the thought of her brought always a voiceless groan. To her, he had let his doubts be known, and her white silence closed his own lips then and there. The simple fact

that he had doubts was an entering wedge of cold-
ness between them that Chad saw must force them
apart; for he knew that the truth must come soon,
and what would be the bitter cost of that truth. She
could never see him as she saw Harry. Harry was a
beloved and erring brother. Hatred of slavery had
been cunningly planted in his heart by her father's
own brother, upon whose head the blame for
Harry's sin was set. The boy had been taunted until
his own father's scorn had stirred his proud inde-
pendence into stubborn resistance and intensified
his resolution to do what he pleased and what he
thought was right. But Chad—she would never
understand him. She would never understand his
love for the Government that had once abandoned
her people to savages and forced her State and his to
seek aid from a foreign land. In her eyes, too, he
would be rending the hearts that had been tenderest
to him in all the world: and that was all. Of what
fate she would deal out to him he dared not think. If
he lifted his hand against the South, he must strike at
the heart of all he loved best, to which he owed
most. If against the Union, at the heart of all that
was best in himself. In him the pure spirit that gave
birth to the nation was fighting for life. Ah, God!
what should he do—what should he do?

Bull Run

[JOSEPH A. ALTSHELER]

Harry rose to his feet and shook St. Clair and Langdon. "Up, boys!" he said. "The enemy will soon be here. I can see their bayonets glittering on the hills."

The Invincibles sprang to their feet almost as one man, and soon all the troops of Evans were up and humming like bees. Food and coffee were served to them hastily, but, before the last cup was thrown down, a heavy crash came from one of the hills beyond Bull Run, and a shell, screaming over their heads, burst beyond them. It was quickly followed by another, and then the round shot and shells came in dozens from batteries which had been posted well in the night.

The Southern batteries replied with all their might and the riflemen supported them, sending the bullets in sheets across Bull Run. The battle flamed in fifteen minutes into extraordinary violence. Harry had never before heard such a continuous and terrific thunder. It seemed that the drums of his ears would be smashed in, but over his head he heard the continuous hissing and whirring of steel and lead. The Northern riflemen were at work, too, and it was fortunate for the Invincibles that they were able to lie down, as they poured their fire into the bushes and woods on the opposite bank.

The volume of smoke was so great that they could no longer see the position of the enemy, but Harry believed that so much metal must do great damage. Although he was a lieutenant he had snatched up a rifle dropped by some fallen soldier, and he loaded and fired it so often that the barrel grew hot to his hand. Lying so near the river, most of the hostile fire went over the heads of the Invincibles, but now and then a shell or a cluster of bullets struck among them, and Harry heard groans. But he quickly forgot these sounds as he watched the clouds of smoke and the blaze of fire on the other side of Bull Run.

"They are not trying to force the passage of the bridge! Everything is for the best!" shouted Langdon.

"No, they dare not," shouted St. Clair in reply. "No column could live on that bridge in face of our fire."

It seemed strange to Harry that the Northern troops made no attempt to cross. Why did all this tremendous fire go on so long, and yet not a foe set foot upon the bridge? It seemed to him that it had endured for hours. The sun was rising higher and higher and the day was growing hotter and hotter. It lay with the North to make the first movement to cross Bull Run, and yet no attempt was made.

Colonel Talbot came repeatedly along the line of the Invincibles, and Harry saw that he was growing uneasy. Such a great volume of fire, without any effort to take advantage of it, made the veteran suspicious. He knew that those old comrades of his on the other side of Bull Run would not waste their metal in a mere cannonade and long range rifle fire. There must be something behind it. Presently, with the consent of the commander, he drew the Invincibles back from the river, where they were permitted to cease firing, and to rest for a while on their arms.

But as they drew long breaths and tried to clear the smoke from their throats, a rumor ran down the lines. The attack at the bridge was but a feint. Only a minor portion of the hostile army was there. The greater mass had gone on and had already crossed the river in face of the weak left flank of the Southern army. Beauregard had been outwitted. The Yankees were now in great force on his own side of Bull Run, and it would be a pitched battle, face to face.

The whole line of the Invincibles quivered with excitement, and then Harry saw that the rumor was true, or that their commander at least believed it to be so. The firing stopped entirely and the bugles blew the retreat. All the brigades gathered themselves up and, wild with anger and chagrin, slowly withdrew.

"Why are we retreating?" exclaimed Langdon, angrily. "Not a Yankee set his foot on the bridge! We're not whipped!"

"No," said Harry, "we're not whipped, but if we don't retreat we will be. If fifteen or twenty thousand Yankees struck us on the flank while those fellows are still in front everything would go."

These were young troops, who considered a retreat equivalent to a beating, and fierce murmurs ran along the line. But the officers paid no attention, marching them steadily on, while the artillery rumbled by their side. Both to right and left they heard the sound of firing, and they saw the smoke floating against both horizons, but they paid little attention to it. They were wondering what was in store for them.

"Cheer up, you lads!" cried Colonel Talbot. "You'll get all the fighting you can stand, and it won't be long in coming, either."

They marched only half an hour and then the troops were drawn up on a hill, where the officers rapidly formed them into position. It was none too soon. A long blue line, bristling with cannon on either flank, appeared across the fields. It was Burnside with the bulk of the Northern army moving down upon them. Harry was standing beside Colonel

Talbot, ready to carry his orders, and he heard the veteran say, between his teeth:

"The Yankees have fooled us, and this is the great battle at last."

The two forces looked at each other for a few moments. Elsewhere great guns and rifles were already at work, but the sounds came distantly. On the hill and in the fields there was silence, save for the steady tramp of the advancing Northern troops. Then from the rear of the marching lines suddenly came a burst of martial music. The Northern bands, by a queer inversion, were playing Dixie:

> *"In Dixie's land*
> *I'll take my stand,*
> *To live and die for Dixie.*
> *Look away! Look away!*
> *Down South in Dixie."*

Harry's feet beat to the tune, the wild and thrilling air played for the first time to troops going into battle.

"We must answer that," he said to St. Clair.

"Here comes the answer," said St. Clair, and the Southern bands began to play "The Girl I Left Behind Me." The music entered Harry's veins. He could not look without a quiver upon the great mass of men bearing down upon them, but the strains of fife and drum put courage in him and told him to stand fast. He saw the face of Colonel Talbot grow darker and darker, and he had enough experience himself to know that the odds were heavily against them.

The intense burning sun poured down a flood of light, lighting up the opposing ranks of blue and gray, and gleaming along swords and bayonets. Nearer and nearer came the piercing notes of Dixie.

"They march well," murmured Colonel Talbot, "and they will fight well, too."

He did not know that McDowell himself, the Northern commander, was now before them, driving on his men, but he did know that the courage and skill of his old comrades were for the present in the ascendant. Burnside was at the head of the division and it seemed long enough to wrap the whole Southern command in its folds and crush it.

Scattered rifle shots were heard on either flank, and the young Invincibles began to breathe heavily. Millions of black specks danced before them in the hot sunshine, and their nervous ears magnified every sound tenfold.

"I wish that tune the Yankees are playing was ours," said Tom Langdon. "I think I could fight battles by it."

"Then we'll have to capture it," said Harry.

Now the time for talking ceased. The rifle fire on the flanks was rising to a steady rattle, and then came the heavy boom of the cannon on either side. Once more the air was filled with the shriek of shells and the whistling of rifle bullets. Men were falling fast, and through the rising clouds of smoke Harry saw the blue lines still coming on. It seemed to him that they would be overwhelmed, trampled under foot, routed, but he heard Colonel Talbot shouting:

"Steady, Invincibles! Steady!"

And Lieutenant-Colonel St. Hilaire, walking up and down the lines, also uttered the same shout. But the blue line never ceased coming. Harry could see the faces dark with sweat and dust and powder still pressing on. It was well for the Southerners that nearly all of them had been trained in the use of the rifle, and it was well for them, too, that most of their officers were men of skill and experience. Recruits, they stood fast nevertheless and their rifles sent the bullets in an unceasing bitter hail straight into the advancing ranks of blue. There was no sound from the bands now. If they were playing somewhere in the rear no one heard. The fire of the cannon and rifles was a steady roll, louder than thunder and more awful.

The Northern troops hesitated at last in face of such a resolute stand and such accurate firing. Then they retreated a little and a shout of triumph came from the Southern lines, but the respite was only for a moment. The men in blue came on again, walking over their dead and past their wounded.

"If they keep pressing in, and it looks as if they would, they will crush us," murmured Colonel Talbot, but he did not let the Invincibles hear him say it. He encouraged them with voice and example, and they bent forward somewhat to meet the second charge of the Northern army, which was now coming. The smoke lifted a little and Harry saw the green fields and the white house of the Widow Henry standing almost in the middle of the battlefield, but unharmed. Then his eyes came back to the hostile line, which, torn by shot and shell, had closed up, nevertheless, and was advancing again in overwhelming force.

Harry now had a sudden horrible fear that they would be trodden under foot. He looked at St. Clair and saw that his face was ghastly. Langdon had long since ceased to smile or utter words of happy philosophy.

"Open up and let the guns through!" someone suddenly cried, and a wild cheer of relief burst from the Invincibles as they made a path. The valiant Bee and Bartow, rushing to the sound of the great firing, had come with nearly three thousand men and a whole battery. Never were men more welcome. They formed instantly along the Southern front, and the battery opened at once with all its guns, while the three thousand men sent a new fire into the Northern ranks. Yet the Northern charge still came. McDowell, Burnside, and the others were pressing it home, seeking to drive the Southern army from its hill, while they were yet able to bring forces largely superior to bear upon it.

The thunder and crash of the terrible conflict rolled over all the hills and fields for miles. It told the other forces of either army that here was the center of the battle, and here was its crisis. The sounds reached an extraordinary young-old man, bearded and awkward, often laughed at, but never to be laughed at again, one of the most wonderful soldiers the world has ever produced, and instantly gathering up his troops he rushed them toward the very heart of the combat. Stonewall Jackson was about to receive his famous nickname.

Jackson's burning eyes swept proudly over the ranks of his tall Virginians, who mourned every second they lost from the battle. An officer retreating with his battery glanced at him, opened his mouth to speak, but closed it again without saying a word, and infused with new hope, turned his guns afresh toward the enemy. Already men were feeling the magnetic current of energy and resolution that flowed from Jackson like water from a fountain.

A message from Colonel Talbot, which he was to deliver to Jackson himself, sent Harry to the rear. He rode a borrowed horse and he galloped rapidly until he saw a long line of men marching forward at a swift but steady pace. At their head rode a man on a sorrel horse. His shoulders were stooped a little, and he leaned forward in the saddle, gazing intently at the vast bank of smoke and flame before him. Harry noticed that the hands upon the bridle reins did not twitch nor did the horseman seem at all excited. Only his burning eyes showed that every faculty was concentrated upon the task. Harry was conscious even then that he was in the presence of General Jackson.

The boy delivered his message. Jackson received it without comment, never taking his eyes from the battle, which was now raging so fiercely in front of them. Behind came his great brigade of Virginians, the smoke and flame of the battle entering their blood and making their hearts pound fast as they moved forward with increasing speed.

Harry rode back with the young officers of his staff, and now they saw men dash out of the smoke and run toward them. They cried that everything was lost. The lip of Jackson curled in contempt. The long line of his Virginians stopped the fugitives and drove them back to the battle. It was evident to Harry, young as he was, that Jackson would be just in time.

Then they saw a battery galloping from that bank of smoke and flame, and, its officer swearing violently, exclaimed that he had been left without support. The stern face and somber eyes of Jackson were turned upon him.

"Unlimber your guns at once," he said. "Here is your support."

Then the valiant Bee himself came, covered with dust, his clothes torn by bullets, his horse in a white lather. He, too, turned to that stern brown figure, as unflinching as death itself, and he cried that the enemy in overwhelming numbers were beating them back.

"Then," said Jackson, "we'll close up and give them the bayonet."

His teeth shut down like a vise. Again the electric current leaped forth and sparkled through the veins of Bee, who turned and rode back into the Southern throng, the Virginians following swiftly. Then Jackson looked over the field with the eye and mind of genius, the eye that is able to see and the mind that is able to understand amid all the thunder and confusion and excitement of battle.

He saw a stretch of pines on the edge of the hill near the Henry house. He quickly marched his troops among the trees, covering their front with six cannon, while the great horseman, Stuart, plumed and eager, formed his cavalry upon the left. Harry felt instinctively that the battle was about to be restored for the time at least, and he turned back to Colonel Talbot and the Invincibles. A shell burst near him. A piece struck his horse in the chest, and Harry felt the animal quiver under him. Then the horse uttered a terrible neighing cry, but Harry, alert and agile, sprang clear, and ran back to his own command.

On the other side of Bull Run was the Northern command of Tyler, which had been rebuffed so fiercely three days before. It, too, heard the roar and crash of the battle, and sought a way across Bull

Run, but for a time could find none. An officer named Sherman, also destined for a mighty fame, saw a Confederate trooper riding across the river further down, and instantly the whole command charged at the ford. It was defended by only two hundred Southern skirmishers whom they brushed out of the way. They were across in a few minutes, and then they advanced on a run to swell McDowell's army. The forces on both sides were increasing and the battle was rising rapidly in volume. But in the face of repeated and furious attacks the Southern troops held fast to the little plateau. Young's Branch flowed on one side of it and protected them in a measure; but only the indomitable spirit of Jackson and Evans, of Bee and Bartow, and others kept them in line against those charges which threatened to shiver them to pieces.

"Look!" cried Bee to some of his men who were wavering. "Look at Jackson, standing there like a stone wall!"

The men ceased to waver and settled themselves anew for a fresh attack.

But in spite of everything the Northern army was gaining ground. Sherman at the very head of the fresh forces that had crossed Bull Run hurled himself upon the Southern army, his main attack falling directly upon the Invincibles. The young recruits reeled, but Colonel Talbot and Lieutenant-Colonel St. Hilaire still ran up and down the lines begging them to stand. They took fresh breath and planted their feet deep once more. Harry raised his rifle and took aim at a flitting figure in the smoke. Then he dropped the muzzle. Either it was reality or a powerful trick of the fancy. It was his own cousin, Dick Mason, but the smoke closed in again, and he did not see the face.

The rush of Sherman was met and repelled. He drew back only to come again, and along the whole line the battle closed in once more, fiercer and more deadly than ever. Upon all the combatants beat the fierce sun of July, and clouds of dust rose to mingle with the smoke of cannon and rifles.

The advantage now lay distinctly with the Northern army, won by its clever passage of Bull Run and surprise. But the courage and tenacity of the Southern troops averted defeat and rout in detail. Jackson, in his strong position near the Henry house, in the cellars of which women were hiding, refused to give an inch of ground. Beauregard, called by the cannon, arrived upon the field only an hour before noon, meeting on the way many fugitives, whom he and his officers drove back into the battle. Hampton's South Carolina Legion, which reached Richmond only that morning, came by train and landed directly upon the battlefield about noon. In five minutes it was in the thick of the battle, and it alone stemmed a terrific rush of Sherman, when all others gave way.

Noon had passed and the heart of McDowell swelled with exultation. The Northern troops were still gaining ground, and at many points the Southern line was crushed. Some of the recruits in gray, their nerves shaken horribly, were beginning to run. But fresh troops coming up met them and turned them back to the field. Beauregard and Johnston, the two senior generals, both experienced and calm, were reforming their ranks, seizing new and strong positions, and hurrying up every portion of their force. Johnston himself, after the first rally, hurried back for fresh regiments, while Jackson's men not only held their ground but began to drive the Northern troops before them.

The Invincibles had fallen back somewhat, leaving many dead behind them. Many more were wounded. Harry had received two bullets through his clothing, and St. Clair was nicked on the wrist. Colonel Talbot and Lieutenant-Colonel St. Hilaire were still unharmed, but a deep gloom had settled over the Invincibles. They had not been beaten, but certainly they were not winning. Their ranks were seamed and rent. From the place where they now stood they could see the place where they formerly stood, but Northern troops occupied it now. Tears ran down the faces of some of the youngest, streaking the dust and powder into hideous, grinning masks.

Harry threw himself upon the ground and lay there for a few moments, panting. He choked with heat and thirst, and his heart seemed to have swollen so much within him that it would be a relief to have it burst. His eyes burned with the dust and smoke, and all about him was a fearful reek. He could see from where he lay most of the battlefield. He saw the Northern batteries fire, move forward, and then fire again. He saw the Northern infantry creeping up, ever creeping, and far behind he beheld the flags of fresh regiments coming to their aid. The tears sprang to his eyes. It seemed in very truth that all was lost. In another part of the field the men in blue had seized the Robinson house, and from points near it their artillery was searching the Southern ranks. A sudden grim humor seized the boy.

"Tom," he shouted to Langdon, "what was that you said about sleeping in the White House at Washington with your boots on?"

"I said it," Langdon shouted back, "but I guess it's all off! For God's sake, Harry, give me a drink of water! I'll give anybody a million dollars and a half dozen states for a single drink!"

A soldier handed him a canteen, and he drank from it. The water was warm, but it was nectar, and when he handed it back, he said:

"I don't know you and you don't know me, but if I could I'd give you a whole lake in return for this. Harry, what are our chances?"

"I don't know. We've lost one battle, but we may have time to win another. Jackson and those

Virginians of his seem able to stand anything. Up, boys, the battle is on us again!"

The charge swept almost to their feet, but it was driven back, and then came a momentary lull, not a cessation of the battle, but merely a sinking, as if the combatants were gathering themselves afresh for a new and greater effort. It was two o'clock in the afternoon, and the fierce July sun was at its zenith, pouring its burning rays upon both armies, alike upon the living and upon the dead who were now so numerous.

The lull was most welcome to the men in gray. Some fresh regiments sent by Johnston had come already, and they hoped for more, but whether they came or not, the army must stand. The brigades were massed heavily around the Henry house with that of Jackson standing stern and indomitable, the strongest wall against the foe. His fame and his spirit were spreading fast over the field.

The lull was brief, the whole Northern army, its lines reformed, swept forward in a half curve, and the Southern army sent forth a stream of shells and bullets to meet it. The brigades of Jackson and Sherman, indomitable foes, met face to face and swept back and forth over the ground, which was littered with their fallen. Everywhere the battle assumed a closer and fiercer phase. Hampton, who had come just in time with his guns, went down wounded badly. Beauregard himself was wounded slightly, and so was Jackson, hit in the hand. Many distinguished officers were killed.

The whole Northern army was driven back four times, and it came a fifth time to be repulsed once more. In the very height of the struggle Harry caught a glimpse in front of them of a long horizontal line of red, like a gleaming ribbon.

"It's those Zouaves!" cried Langdon. "Shoot their pants!"

He did not mean it as a jest. The words just jumped out, and true to their meaning the Invincibles fired straight at that long line of red, and then reloading fired again. The Zouaves were cut to pieces, the field was strewed with their brilliant uniforms. A few officers tried to bring on the scattered remnants, but two regiments of regulars, sweeping in between and bearing down on the Invincibles, saved them from extermination.

The Invincibles would have suffered the fate they had dealt out to the Zouaves, but fresh regiments came to their help and the regulars were driven back. Sherman and Jackson were still fighting face to face, and Sherman was unable to advance. Howard hurled a fresh force on the men in gray. Bee and Bartow, who had done such great deeds earlier in the day, were both killed. A Northern force under Heintzelman, converging for a flank attack, was set upon and routed by the Southerners, who put them all to flight, captured three guns and took the Robinson house.

Fortune, nevertheless, still seemed to favor the North. The Southerners had barely held their positions around the Henry house. Most of their cannon were dismounted. Hundreds had dropped from exhaustion. Some had died from heat and excessive exertion. The mortality among the officers was frightful. There were few hopeful hearts in the Southern army.

It was now three o'clock in the afternoon and Beauregard, through his glasses, saw a great column of dust rising above the tops of the trees. His experience told him that it must be made by marching troops, but what troops were they, Northern or Southern? In an agony of suspense he appealed to the generals around him, but they could tell nothing. He sent off aides at a gallop to see, but meanwhile he and his generals could only wait, while the column of dust grew broader and broader and higher and higher. His heart sank like a plummet in a pool. The cloud was on the Federal flank and everything indicated that it was the army of Patterson, marching from the Valley of Virginia.

Harry and his comrades had also seen the dust, and they regarded it anxiously. They knew as well as any general present that their fate lay within that cloud.

"It's coming fast, and it's growing faster," said Harry. "I've got so used to the roar of this battle that it seems to me alien sounds are detached from it, and are heard easily. I can hear the rumble of cannon wheels in that cloud."

"Then tell us, Harry," said Langdon, "is it a North-ern rumble or a Southern rumble that you hear?"

Harry laughed.

"I'll admit it's a good deal of a fancy," he said.

Arthur St. Clair suddenly leaped high in the air, and uttered at the very top of his voice the wild note of the famous rebel yell.

"Look at the flags aloft in that cloud of dust! It's the Stars and Bars! God bless the Bonnie Blue Flag! They are our own men coming, and coming in time!"

Now the battle flags appeared clearly through the dust, and the great rebel yell, swelling and tri-umphant, swept the whole Southern line. It was the remainder of Johnston's Army of the Shenandoah. It had slipped away from Patterson, and all through the burning day it had been marching steadily toward the battlefield, drummed on by the thudding guns. Johnston, the silent and alert, was himself with them now, and aflame with zeal they were advancing on the run straight for the heart of the Northern army.

Kirby Smith, one of Harry's own Kentucky gen-erals, was in the very van of the relieving force. A man after Stonewall Jackson's own soul, he rushed forward with the leading regiments and they hurled themselves bodily upon the Northern flank.

The impact was terrible. Smith fell wounded, but his men rushed on and the men behind also threw themselves into the battle. Almost at the same instant Jubal Early, who had made a circuit with a strong force, hurled it upon the side of the Northern army. The brave troops in blue were exhausted by so many hours of fierce fighting and fierce heat. Their whole line broke and began to fall back. The Southern generals around the Henry house saw it and exulted. Swift orders were sent and the bugles blew the charge for the men who had stood so many long and bitter hours on the defense.

"Now, Invincibles, now!" cried Colonel Leonidas Talbot. "Charge home, just once, my boys, and the victory is ours!"

Covered with dust and grime, worn and bleeding with many wounds, but every heart beating triumphantly, what was left of the Invincibles rose up and followed their leader. Harry was conscious of a flame almost in his face and of whirling clouds of smoke and dust. Then the entire Southern army burst upon the confused Northern force and shattered it so completely that it fell to pieces.

The bravest battle ever fought by men, who, with few exceptions, had not smelled the powder of war before, was lost and won.

As the Southern cannon and rifles beat upon them, the Northern army, save for the regulars and the cavalry, dissolved. The generals could not stem the flood. They rushed forward in confused masses, seeking only to save themselves. Whole regiments dashed into the fords of Bull Run and emerged dripping on the other side. A bridge was covered with spectators come out from Washington to see the victory, many of them bringing with them baskets of lunch. Some were Members of Congress, but all joined in the panic and flight, carrying to the capital many untrue stories of disaster.

A huge mass of fleeing men emerged upon the Warrenton turnpike, throwing away their weapons and ammunition that they might run the faster. It was panic pure and simple, but panic for the day only. For hours they had fought as bravely as the veterans of twenty battles, but now, with weakened nerves, they thought that an overwhelming force was upon them. Every shell that the Southern guns sent among them urged them to greater speed. The cavalry and little force of regulars covered the rear, and with firm and unbroken ranks retreated slowly, ready to face the enemy if he tried pursuit.

But the men in gray made no real pursuit. They were so worn that they could not follow, and they yet scarcely believed in the magnitude of their own victory, snatched from the very jaws of defeat. Twenty-eight Northern cannon and ten flags were in their hands, but thousands of dead and wounded lay upon the field, and night was at hand again, close and hot.

Harry turned back to the little plateau where those that were left of the Invincibles were already kindling their cooking fires. He looked for his two comrades and recognized them both under their masks of dust and powder.

"Are you hurt, Tom?" he said to Langdon.

"No, and I'm going to sleep in the White House at Washington after all."

"And you, Arthur?"

"There's a red line across my wrist, where a bullet passed, but it's nothing. Listen, what do you think of that, boys?"

A Southern band had gathered in the edge of the wood and was playing a wild thrilling air, the words of which meant nothing, but the tune everything:

> *"In Dixie's land*
> *I'll take my stand,*
> *To live and die for Dixie.*
> *Look away! Look away!*
> *Look away down South in Dixie."*

"So we have taken their tune from them and made it ours!" St. Clair exclaimed jubilantly. "After all, it really belonged to us! We'll play it through the streets of Washington."

But Colonel Leonidas Talbot, who stood close by, raised his hand warningly.

"Boys," he said, "this is only the beginning."

The Tedium of Camp

[JOHN MCELROY]

To really enjoy life in a Camp of Instruction requires a peculiar cast of mind. It requires a genuine liking for a tread-mill round of merely mechanical duties; it requires a taste for rising in the chill and cheerless dawn, at the unwelcome summons of "reveille," to a long day filled with a tiresome routine of laborious drills alternating with tedious roll-calls, and wearisome parades and inspections; it requires pleased contentment with walks continually cut short by the camp-guard, and with amusements limited to rough horse-play on the parade-ground, and dull games of cards by sputtering candles in the tent.

As these be tastes and preferences notably absent from the mind of the average young man, our volunteers usually regard their experience in Camp of

Instruction as among the most unpleasant of their war memories.

These were the trials that tested Harry Glen's resolution sorely. When he enlisted with the intention of redeeming himself, he naturally expected that the opportunity he desired would be given by a prompt march to the field, and a speedy entrance into an engagement. He nerved himself strenuously for the dreadful ordeal of battle, but this became a continually receding point. The bitter defeat at Bull Run was bearing fruit in months of painstaking preparation before venturing upon another collision.

Day by day he saw the chance of retrieving his reputation apparently more remote. Meanwhile discouragements and annoyances grew continually more plentiful and irksome. He painfully learned that the most disagreeable part of war is not the trial of battle, but the daily sacrifices of personal liberty, tastes, feelings and conveniences involved in camp-life, and in the reduction of one's cherished individuality to the dead-level of a passive, obedient, will-less private soldier.

"I do wish the regiment would get orders to move!" said almost hourly each one of a half-million impatient youths fretting in Camps of Instruction through the long Summer of 1861.

"I do wish the regiment would get orders to move!" said Harry Glen angrily one evening, on coming into the Surgeon's tent to have his blistered hands dressed. He had been on fatigue duty during the day, and the Fatigue-Squad had had an obstinate struggle with an old oak stump, which disfigured the parade-ground, and resisted removal like an Irish tenant.

"I am willing—yes, I can say I am anxious, even— to go into battle," he continued, while Dr. Paul Denslow laid plasters of simple cerate on the abraded palms, and then swathed them in bandages. "Anything is preferable to this chopping tough stumps with a dull ax, and drilling six hours a day while the thermometer hangs around the nineties."

"I admit that there are things which would seem pleasanter to a young man of your temperament and previous habits," said the Surgeon, kindly. "Shift over into that arm-stool, which you will find easier, and rest a little while. Julius, bring in that box of cigars."

While Julius, who resembled his illustrious name-sake as little in celerity of movement as he did in complexion, was coming, the Surgeon prepared a paper, which he presented to Harry, saying:

"There, that'll keep you off duty to-morrow. After that, we'll see what can be done."

Julius arrived with the cigars as tardily as if he had had to cross a Rubicon in the back room. Two were lighted, and the Surgeon settled himself for a chat.

"Have you become tired of soldier-life?" asked he, studying Harry's face for the effect of the question.

"I cannot say that I have become tired of it," said Harry, frankly, "because I must admit that I never had the slightest inclination to it. I had less fancy for becoming a soldier than for any other honorable pursuit that you could mention."

"Then you only joined the army—"

"From a sense of duty merely," said Harry, knocking the ashes from his cigar.

"And the physical and other discomforts now begin to weight nearly as much as that sense of duty?"

"Not at all. It only seems to me that there are more of them than are absolutely essential to the performance of that duty. I want to be of service to the country, but I would prefer that that service be not made unnecessarily onerous."

"Quite natural; quite natural."

"For example, how have the fatigues and pains of my afternoon's chopping contributed a particle toward the suppression of the rebellion? What have my blistered hands to do with the hurts of actual conflict?"

"Let us admit that the connection is somewhat obscure," said Doctor Denslow, philosophically.

"It is easier for you, than for me, to view the matter calmly. Your hands are unhurt. I am the galled jade whose withers are wrung."

"Body and spirit both bruised?" said the Surgeon, half reflectively.

Harry colored. "Yes," he said, rather defiantly. "In

addition to desiring to serve my country, I want to vindicate my manhood from some aspersions which have been cast upon it."

"Quite a fair showing of motives. Better, perhaps, than usual, when a careful weighing of the relative proportions of self-esteem, self-interest and higher impulses is made."

"I am free to say that the discouragements I have met with are very different, and perhaps much greater than I contemplated. Nor can I bring myself to believe that they are necessary. I am trying to be entirely willing to peril life and limb on the field of battle, but instead of placing me where I can do this, and allowing me to concentrate all my energies upon that object, I am kept for months chafing under the petty tyrannies of a bullying officer, and deprived of most of the comforts that I have heretofore regarded as necessary to my existence. What good can be accomplished by diverting forces which should be devoted to the main struggle into this ignoble channel? That's what puzzles and irritates me."

"It seems to be one of the inseparable conditions of the higher forms of achievement that they require vastly more preparation for them than the labor of doing them."

"That's no doubt very philosophical, but it's not satisfactory, for all that."

"My dear boy, learn this grand truth now: That philosophy is never satisfactory; it is only mitigatory.

It consists mainly in saying with many fine words: 'What can't be cured must be endured.'"

"I presume that is so. I wish, though, that by the mere saying so, I could make the endurance easier."

"I can make your lot in the service easier."

"Indeed! How so?"

"By having you appointed my Hospital Steward. I have not secured one yet, and the man who is acting as such is so intemperate that I feel a fresh sense of escape with every day that passes without his mistaking the oxalic acid for Epsom salts, to the destruction of some earnest but constipated young patriot's whole digestive viscera.

"If you accept this position," continued the Surgeon, flinging away his refractory cigar in disgust, and rising to get a fresh one, "you will have the best rank and pay of any non-commissioned officer in the regiment; better, indeed, than that of a Second Lieutenant. You will have your quarters here with me, and be compelled to associate with no one but me, thus reducing your disagreeable companions at a single stroke, to one. And you will escape finally from all subserviency to Lieutenant Alspaugh, or indeed to any other officer in the regiment, except your humble servant. As to food, you will mess with me."

"Those are certainly very strong inducements," said Harry, meditating upon the delightfulness of relief from the myriad of rasping little annoyances which rendered every day of camp-life an infliction.

"Yes, and still further, you will never need to go under fire, or expose yourself to danger of any kind, unless you choose to."

Harry's face crimsoned to the hue of the western sky where the sun was just going down. He started to answer hotly, but an understanding of the Surgeon's evident kindness and sincerity interposed to deter him. He knew there was no shaft of sarcasm hidden below this plain speech, and after a moment's consideration he replied:

"I am very grateful, I assure you, for your kindness in this matter. I am strongly tempted to accept your offer, but there are still stronger reasons why I should decline it."

"May I ask your reasons?"

"My reasons for not accepting the appointment?"

"Yes, the reasons which impel you to prefer a dinner of bitter herbs, under Mr. Alspaugh's usually soiled thumb, to a stalled ox and my profitable society," said the Surgeon, gayly.

Harry hesitated a moment, and then decided to speak frankly. "Yes," he said, "your kindness gives you the right to know. To not tell you would show a lack of gratitude. I made a painful blunder before in not staying unflinchingly with my company. The more I think of it, the more I regret it, and the more I am decided not to repeat it, but abide with my comrades and share their fate in all things. I feel that I no longer have a choice in the matter; I must do it. But there goes the drum for roll-call. I must go. Good evening, and very many thanks."

"The young fellow's no callow milksop, after all," said the Surgeon Denslow, as his eyes followed Harry's retreating form. "His gristle is hardening into something like his stern old father's backbone."

What I Saw of Shiloh

[**AMBROSE BIERCE**]

I

This is a simple story of a battle; such a tale as may be told by a soldier who is no writer to a reader who is no soldier.

The morning of Sunday, the sixth day of April, 1862, was bright and warm. Reveille had been sounded rather late, for the troops, wearied with long marching, were to have a day of rest. The men were idling about the embers of their bivouac fires; some preparing breakfast, others looking carelessly to the condition of their arms and accoutrements, against the inevitable inspection; still others were chatting with indolent dogmatism on that never-failing theme, the end and object of the campaign. Sentinels paced up and down the confused front with a lounging freedom of mien and stride that would not have been tolerated at another time. A few of them limped unsoldierly in deference to blistered feet. At a little distance in rear of the stacked arms were a few tents out of which frowsy-headed officers occasionally peered, languidly calling to their servants to fetch a basin of water, dust a coat or polish a scabbard. Trim young mounted orderlies, bearing dispatches obviously unimportant, urged their lazy nags by devious ways amongst the men, enduring with unconcern their good-humored raillery, the penalty of superior station. Little negroes of not very clearly defined status and function lolled on their stomachs, kicking their long, bare heels in the sunshine, or slumbered peacefully, unaware of the practical waggery prepared by white hands for their undoing.

Presently the flag hanging limp and lifeless at headquarters was seen to lift itself spiritedly from the staff. At the same instant was heard a dull, distant sound like the heavy breathing of some great animal below the horizon. The flag had lifted its head to listen. There was a momentary lull in the hum of the human swarm; then, as the flag drooped the hush passed away. But there were some hundreds more men on their feet than before; some thousands of hearts beating with a quicker pulse.

Again the flag made a warning sign, and again the breeze bore to our ears the long, deep sighing of iron lungs. The division, as if it had received the sharp word of command, sprang to its feet, and stood in groups at "attention." Even the little blacks got up. I have since seen similar effects produced by earthquakes; I am not sure but the ground was trembling then. The mess-cooks, wise in their generation, lifted the steaming camp-kettles off the fire and stood by to cast out. The mounted orderlies had somehow disappeared. Officers came ducking from beneath their tents and gathered in groups. Headquarters had become a swarming hive.

The sound of the great guns now came in regular throbbings—the strong, full pulse of the fever of battle. The flag flapped excitedly, shaking out its blazonry of stars and stripes with a sort of fierce delight. Toward the knot of officers in its shadow dashed from somewhere—he seemed to have burst out of the ground in a cloud of dust—a mounted aide-de-camp, and on the instant rose the sharp, clear notes of a bugle, caught up and repeated, and passed on by other bugles, until the level reaches of brown fields, the line of woods trending away to far hills, and the unseen valleys beyond were "telling of the sound," the farther, fainter strains half drowned in ringing cheers as the men ran to range themselves behind the stacks of arms. For this call was not the wearisome "general" before which the tents go down; it was the exhilarating "assembly," which goes to the heart as wine and stirs the blood like the kisses of a beautiful woman. Who that has heard it calling to him above the grumble of great guns can forget the wild intoxication of its music?

II

The Confederate forces in Kentucky and Tennessee had suffered a series of reverses, culminating in the loss of Nashville. The blow was severe: immense quantities of war material had fallen to the victor, together with all the important strategic points. General Johnston withdrew Beauregard's army to Corinth, in northern Mississippi, where he hoped so to recruit and equip it as to enable it to assume the offensive and retake the lost territory.

The town of Corinth was a wretched place—the capital of a swamp. It is two days' march west of the Tennessee River, which here and for a hundred and fifty miles farther, to where it falls into the Ohio at Paducah, runs nearly north. It is navigable to this point—that is to say, to Pittsburg Landing, where Corinth got to it by a road worn through a thickly wooded country seamed with ravines and bayous, rising nobody knows where and running into the river under sylvan arches heavily draped with Spanish moss. In some places they were obstructed by fallen trees. The Corinth road was at certain seasons a branch of the Tennessee River. Its mouth was Pittsburg Landing. Here in 1862 were some fields and a house or two; now there are a national cemetery and other improvements.

It was at Pittsburg Landing that Grant established his army, with a river in his rear and two toy

steamboats as a means of communication with the
east side, whither General Buell with thirty thousand
men was moving from Nashville to join him. The
question has been asked, Why did General Grant
occupy the enemy's side of the river in the face of
a superior force before the arrival of Buell? Buell
had a long way to come; perhaps Grant was weary
of waiting. Certainly Johnston was, for in the gray
of the morning of April 6th, when Buell's leading
division was en bivouac near the little town of
Savannah, eight or ten miles below, the Confederate forces, having moved out of Corinth two days
before, fell upon Grant's advance brigades and
destroyed them. Grant was at Savannah, but hastened to the Landing in time to find his camps in the
hands of the enemy and the remnants of his beaten
army cooped up with an impassable river at their
backs for moral support. I have related how the
news of this affair came to us at Savannah. It came
on the wind—a messenger that does not bear
copious details.

III

On the side of the Tennessee River, over against
Pittsburg Landing, are some low bare hills, partly
inclosed by a forest. In the dusk of the evening of
April 6 this open space, as seen from the other side
of the stream—whence, indeed, it was anxiously
watched by thousands of eyes, to many of which it

grew dark long before the sun went down—would have appeared to have been ruled in long, dark lines, with new lines being constantly drawn across. These lines were the regiments of Buell's leading division, which having moved from Savannah through a country presenting nothing but interminable swamps and pathless "bottom lands," with rank overgrowths of jungle, was arriving at the scene of action breathless, footsore and faint with hunger. It had been a terrible race; some regiments had lost a third of their number from fatigue, the men dropping from the ranks as if shot, and left to recover or die at their leisure. Nor was the scene to which they had been invited likely to inspire the moral confidence that medicines physical fatigue. True, the air was full of thunder and the earth was trembling beneath their feet; and if there is truth in the theory of the conversion of force, these men were storing up energy from every shock that burst its waves upon their bodies. Perhaps this theory may better than another explain the tremendous endurance of men in battle. But the eyes reported only matter for despair.

Before us ran the turbulent river, vexed with plunging shells and obscured in spots by blue sheets of low-lying smoke. The two little steamers were doing their duty well. They came over to us empty and went back crowded, sitting very low in the water, apparently on the point of capsizing. The farther edge of the water could not be seen; the boats came out of the obscurity, took on their passengers and vanished in the darkness. But on the heights above, the battle was burning brightly enough; a thousand lights kindled and expired in every second of time. There were broad flushings in the sky, against which the branches of the trees showed black. Sudden flames burst out here and there, singly and in dozens. Fleeting streaks of fire crossed over to us by way of welcome. These expired in blinding flashes and fierce little rolls of smoke, attended with the peculiar metallic ring of bursting shells, and followed by the musical humming of the fragments as they struck into the ground on every side, making us wince, but doing little harm. The air was full of noises. To the right and the left the musketry rattled smartly and petulantly; directly in front it sighed and growled. To the experienced ear this meant that the death-line was an arc of which the river was the chord. There were deep, shaking explosions and smart shocks; the whisper of stray bullets and the hurtle of conical shells; the rush of round shot. There were faint, desultory cheers, such as announce a momentary or partial triumph. Occasionally, against the glare behind the trees, could be seen moving black figures, singularly distinct but apparently no longer than a thumb. They seemed to me ludicrously like the figures of demons in old allegorical prints of hell. To destroy these and all their belongings the enemy needed but another hour of daylight; the steamers in that case would have been doing him fine service by bringing more fish to his net. Those of us who had the good fortune to arrive late could then have eaten our teeth in important rage. Nay, to make his victory sure it did not need that the sun should pause in the heavens; one of many random shots falling into the river would have done the business had chance directed it into the engine-room of a steamer. You can perhaps fancy the anxiety with which we watched them leaping down.

But we had two other allies besides the night. Just where the enemy had pushed his right flank to the river was the mouth of a wide bayou, and here two gunboats had taken station. They too were of the toy sort, plated perhaps with railway metals, perhaps with boiler-iron. They staggered under a heavy gun or two each. The bayou made an opening in the high bank of the river. The bank was a parapet, behind which the gunboats crouched, firing up the bayou as through an embrasure. The enemy was at this disadvantage: he could not get at the gunboats, and he could advance only by exposing his flank to their ponderous missiles, one of which would have broken a half-mile of his bones and made nothing of it. Very annoying this must have been—these twenty gunners beating back an army because a sluggish creek had been pleased to fall into a river at one point rather than another. Such is the part that accident may play in the game of war.

As a spectacle this was rather fine. We could just discern the black bodies of these boats, looking very much like turtles. But when they let off their big guns there was a conflagration. The river shuddered in its banks, and hurried on, bloody, wounded, terrified! Objects a mile away sprang toward our eyes as a snake strikes at the face of its victim. The report stung us to the brain, but we blessed it audibly. Then we could hear the great shell tearing away through the air until the sound died out in the distance; then, a surprisingly long time afterward, a dull, distant explosion and a sudden silence of small-arms told their own tale.

IV

There was, I remember, no elephant on the boat that passed us across that evening, nor, I think, any hippopotamus. These would have been out of place. We had, however, a woman. Whether the baby was somewhere on board I did not learn. She was a fine creature, this woman; somebody's wife. Her mission, as she understood it, was to inspire the failing heart with courage; and when she selected mine I felt less flattered by her preference than astonished by her penetration. How did she learn? She stood on the upper deck with the red blaze of battle bathing her beautiful face, the twinkle of a thousand rifles mirrored in her eyes; and displaying a small ivory-handled pistol, she told me in a sentence punctuated by the thunder of great guns that if it came to the worst she would do her duty like a man! I am proud to remember that I took off my hat to this little fool.

V

Along the sheltered strip of beach between the river bank and the water was a confused mass of humanity—several thousands of men. They were mostly unarmed; many were wounded; some dead. All the camp-following tribes were there; all the cowards; a few officers. Not one of them knew where his regiment was, nor if he had a regiment. Many had not. These men were defeated, beaten, cowed. They were deaf to duty and dead to shame. A more demented crew never drifted to the rear of broken battalions. They would have stood in their tracks and been shot down to a man by a provost-marshal's guard, but they could not have been urged up that bank. An army's bravest men are its cowards. The death which they would not meet at the hands of the enemy they will meet at the hands of their officers, with never a flinching.

Whenever a steamboat would land, this abominable mob had to be kept off her with bayonets; when she pulled away, they sprang on her and were pushed by scores into the water, where they were suffered to drown one another in their own way. The men disembarking insulted them, shoved them, struck them. In return they expressed their unholy delight in the certainty of our destruction by the enemy.

By the time my regiment had reached the plateau night had put an end to the struggle. A sputter of rifles would break out now and then, followed perhaps by a spiritless hurrah. Occasionally a shell from a far-away battery would come pitching down somewhere near, with a whir crescendo, or flit above our heads with a whisper like that made by the wings of a night bird, to smother itself in the river. But there was no more fighting. The gunboats, however, blazed away at set intervals all night long, just to make the enemy uncomfortable and break him of his rest.

For us there was no rest. Foot by foot we moved through the dusky fields, we knew not whither. There were men all about us, but no camp-fires; to have made a blaze would have been madness. The men were of strange regiments; they mentioned the names of unknown generals. They gathered in groups by the wayside, asking eagerly our numbers. They recounted the depressing incidents of the day. A thoughtful officer shut their mouths with a sharp word as he passed; a wise one coming after encouraged them to repeat their doleful tale all along the line.

Hidden in hollows and behind clumps of rank brambles were large tents, dimly lighted with candles, but looking comfortable. The kind of comfort they supplied was indicated by pairs of men entering and reappearing, bearing litters; by low moans from within and by long rows of dead with covered faces outside. These tents were constantly receiving the wounded, yet were never full; they were continually ejecting the dead, yet were never empty. It was as if the helpless had been carried in and murdered, that they might not hamper those whose business it was to fall to-morrow.

The night was now black-dark; as is usual after a battle, it had begun to rain. Still we moved; we were being put into position by somebody. Inch by inch we crept along, treading on one another's heels by way of keeping together. Commands were passed along the line in whispers; more commonly none were given. When the men had pressed so closely together that they could advance no farther they stood stock-still, sheltering the locks of their rifles with their ponchos. In this position many fell asleep. When those in front suddenly stepped away those in the rear, roused by the tramping, hastened after with such zeal that the line was soon choked again. Evidently the head of the division was being piloted at a snail's pace by someone who did not feel sure of his ground. Very often we struck our feet against the dead; more frequently against those who still had spirit enough to resent it with a moan. These were lifted carefully to one side and abandoned. Some had sense enough to ask in their weak way for water. Absurd! Their clothes were soaked, their hair dank; their white faces, dimly discernible, were clammy

and cold. Besides, none of us had any water. There
was plenty coming, though, for before midnight a
thunderstorm broke upon us with great violence.
The rain, which had for hours been a dull drizzle, fell
with a copiousness that stifled us; we moved in running water up to our ankles. Happily, we were in a
forest of great trees heavily "decorated" with Spanish
moss, or with an enemy standing to his guns the
disclosures of the lightning might have been incon-
venient. As it was, the incessant blaze enabled us to
consult our watches and encouraged us by displaying our numbers; our black, sinuous line, creeping
like a giant serpent beneath the trees, was apparently
interminable. I am almost ashamed to say how sweet
I found the companionship of those coarse men.

So the long night wore away, and as the glimmer
of morning crept in through the forest we found
ourselves in a more open country. But where?
Not a sign of battle was here. The trees were neither splintered nor scarred, the underbrush was
unmown, the ground had no footprints but our
own. It was as if we had broken into glades sacred
to eternal silence. I should not have been surprised
to see sleek leopards come fawning about our feet,
and milk-white deer confront us with human eyes.

A few inaudible commands from an invisible
leader had placed us in order of battle. But where
was the enemy? Where, too, were the riddled regiments that we had come to save? Had our other

divisions arrived during the night and passed the river to assist us? Or were we to oppose our paltry five thousand breasts to an army flushed with victory? What protected our right? Who lay upon our left? Was there really anything in our front?

There came, borne to us on the raw morning air, the long weird note of a bugle. It was directly before us. It rose with a low clear, deliberate warble, and seemed to float in the gray sky like the note of a lark. The bugle calls of the Federal and the Confederate armies were the same: it was the "assembly"! As it died away I observed that the atmosphere had suffered a change; despite the equilibrium established by the storm, it was electric. Wings were growing on blistered feet. Bruised muscles and jolted bones, shoulders pounded by the cruel knapsack, eyelids leaden from lack of sleep—all were pervaded by the subtle fluid, all were unconscious of their clay. The men thrust forward their heads, expanded their eyes and clenched their teeth. They breathed hard, as if throttled by tugging at the leash. If you had laid your hand in the beard or hair of one of these men it would have crackled and shot sparks.

VI

I suppose the country lying between Corinth and Pittsburg Landing could boast a few inhabitants other than alligators. What manner of people they were it is impossible to say, inasmuch as the fighting dispersed, or possibly exterminated them; perhaps in merely classing them as non-saurian I shall describe them with sufficient particularity and at the same time avert from myself the natural suspicion attaching to a writer who points out to persons who do not know him the peculiarities of persons whom he does not know. One thing, however, I hope I may without offense affirm of these swamp-dwellers— they were pious. To what deity their veneration was given—whether, like the Egyptians, they worshiped the crocodile, or, like other Americans, adored themselves, I do not presume to guess. But whoever, or whatever, may have been the divinity whose ends they shaped, unto Him, or It, they had builded a temple. This humble edifice, centrally situated in the heart of a solitude, and conveniently accessible to the supersylvan crow, had been christened Shiloh Chapel, whence the name of the battle. The fact of a Christian church—assuming it to have been a Christian church—giving name to a wholesale cutting of Christian throats by Christian hands need not be dwelt on here; the frequency of its recurrence in the history of our species has somewhat abated the moral interest that would otherwise attach to it.

VII

Owing to the darkness, the storm and the absence of a road, it had been impossible to move the artillery from the open ground about the Landing.

The privation was much greater in a moral than in a material sense. The infantry soldier feels a confidence in his cumbrous arm quite unwarranted by its actual achievements in thinning out the opposition. There is something that inspires confidence in the way a gun dashes up to the front, shoving fifty or a hundred men to one side as if it said, "Permit me!" Then it squares its shoulders, calmly dislocates a joint in its back, sends away its twenty-four legs and settles down with a quiet rattle which says as plainly as possible, "I've come to stay." There is a superb scorn in its grimly defiant attitude, with its nose in the air; it appears not so much to threaten the enemy as deride him.

Our batteries were probably toiling after us somewhere; we could only hope the enemy might delay his attack until they should arrive. "He may delay his defense if he likes," said a sententious young officer to whom I had imparted this natural wish. He had read the signs aright; the words were hardly spoken when a group of staff officers about the brigade commander shot away in divergent lines as if scattered by a whirlwind, and galloping each to the commander of a regiment gave the word. There was a momentary confusion of tongues, a thin line of skirmishers detached itself from the compact front and pushed forward, followed by its diminutive reserves of half a company each—one of which platoons it was my fortune to command. When the straggling line of skirmishers had swept four or five hundred yards ahead, "See," said one of my comrades, "she moves!" She did indeed, and in fine style, her front as straight as a string, her reserve regiments in columns doubled on the center, following in true subordination; no braying of brass to apprise the enemy, no fifing and drumming to amuse him; no ostentation of gaudy flags; no nonsense. This was a matter of business.

In a few moments we had passed out of the singular oasis that had so marvelously escaped the desolation of battle, and now the evidences of the previous day's struggle were present in profusion. The ground was tolerably level here, the forest less dense, mostly clear of undergrowth, and occasionally opening out into small natural meadows. Here and there were small pools—mere discs of rainwater with a tinge of blood. Riven and torn with cannon-shot, the trunks of the trees protruded bunches of splinters like hands, the fingers above the wound interlacing with those below. Large branches had been lopped, and hung their green heads to the ground, or swung critically in their netting of vines, as in a hammock. Many had been cut clean off and their masses of foliage seriously impeded the progress of the troops. The bark of these trees, from the root upward to a height of ten or twenty feet, was so thickly pierced with bullets and grape that one could not have laid a hand on it without covering several punctures.

None had escaped. How the human body survives a storm like this must be explained by the fact that it is exposed to it but a few moments at a time, whereas these grand old trees had had no one to take their places, from the rising to the going down of the sun. Angular bits of iron, concavo-convex, sticking in the sides of muddy depressions, showed where shells had exploded in their furrows. Knapsacks, canteens, haversacks distended with soaken and swollen biscuits, gaping to disgorge, blankets beaten into the soil by the rain, rifles with bent barrels or splintered stocks, waist-belts, hats and the omnipresent sardine-box—all the wretched debris of the battle still littered the spongy earth as far as one could see, in every direction. Dead horses were everywhere; a few disabled caissons, or limbers, reclining on one elbow, as it were; ammunition wagons standing disconsolate behind four or six sprawling mules. Men? There were men enough; all dead apparently, except one, who lay near where I had halted my platoon to await the slower movement of the line—a Federal sergeant, variously hurt, who had been a fine giant in his time. He lay face upward, taking in his breath in convulsive, rattling snorts, and blowing it out in sputters of froth which crawled creamily down his cheeks, piling itself alongside his neck and ears. A bullet had clipped a groove in his skull, above the temple; from this the brain protruded in bosses, dropping off in flakes and strings. I had not previously known one could get on, even in this unsatisfactory fashion, with so little brain. One of my men whom I knew for a womanish fellow, asked if he should put his bayonet through him. Inexpressibly shocked by the cold-blooded proposal, I told him I thought not; it was unusual, and too many were looking.

VIII

It was plain that the enemy had retreated to Corinth. The arrival of our fresh troops and their successful passage of the river had disheartened him. Three or four of his gray cavalry videttes moving amongst the trees on the crest of a hill in our front, and galloping out of sight at the crack of our skirmishers' rifles, confirmed us in the belief; an army face to face with its enemy does not employ cavalry to watch its front. True, they might be a general and his staff. Crowning this rise we found a level field, a quarter of a mile in width; beyond it a gentle acclivity, covered with an undergrowth of young oaks, impervious to sight. We pushed on into the open, but the division halted at the edge. Having orders to conform to its movements, we halted too; but that did not suit; we received an intimation to proceed. I had performed this sort of service before, and in the exercise of my discretion deployed my platoon, pushing it forward at a run, with trailed arms, to strengthen the skirmish line, which I overtook some thirty or forty yards from the wood. Then—I can't describe it—the forest seemed all at once to flame up and disappear with a crash like that of a great wave upon the beach—a crash that expired in hot hissings, and the sickening "spat" of lead against flesh. A dozen of my brave fellows tumbled over like ten-pins. Some struggled to their feet only to go down again, and yet again. Those who stood fired into the smoking brush and doggedly retired. We had expected to find, at most, a line of skirmishers similar to our own; it was with a view to overcoming them by a sudden coup at the moment of collision that I had thrown forward my little reserve. What we had found was a line of battle, coolly holding its fire till it could count our teeth. There was no more to be done but get back across the open ground, every superficial yard of which was throwing up its little jet of mud provoked by an impinging bullet. We got back, most of us, and I shall never forget the ludicrous incident of a young officer who had taken part in the affair walking up to his colonel, who had been a calm and apparently impartial spectator, and gravely reporting: "The enemy is in force just beyond this field, sir."

I X

In subordination to the design of this narrative, as defined by its title, the incidents related necessarily group themselves about my own personality as a center; and, as this center, during the few terrible hours of the engagement, maintained a variably constant relation to the open field already mentioned, it is important that the reader should bear in mind the topographical and tactical features of the local situation. The hither side of the field was occupied by the front of my brigade—a length of two regiments in line, with proper intervals for field batteries. During the entire fight the enemy held the slight wooded acclivity beyond. The debatable ground to the right and left of the open was broken and thickly wooded for miles, in some places quite inaccessible to artillery and at very few points offering opportunities for its successful employment. As a consequence of this the two sides of the field were soon studded thickly with confronting guns, which flamed away at one another with amazing zeal and rather startling effect. Of course, an infantry attack delivered from either side was not to be thought of when the covered flanks offered inducements so unquestionably superior; and I believe the riddled bodies of my poor skirmishers were the only ones left on this "neutral ground" that day. But there was a very pretty line of dead continually growing in our rear, and doubtless the enemy had at his back a similar encouragement.

The configuration of the ground offered us no protection. By lying flat on our faces between the guns we were screened from view by a straggling row of brambles, which marked the course of an obsolete fence; but the enemy's grape was sharper than his eyes, and it was poor consolation to know that his gunners could not see what they were doing, so long as they did it. The shock of our own pieces nearly deafened us, but in the brief intervals we could hear the battle roaring and stammering in the dark reaches of the forest to the right and left, where our other divisions were dashing themselves again and again into the smoking jungle. What would we not have given to join them in their brave, hopeless task! But to lie inglorious beneath showers of shrapnel darting divergent from the unassailable sky—meekly to be blown out of life by level gusts of grape—to clench our teeth and shrink helpless before big shot pushing noisily through the consenting air— this was horrible! "Lie down, there!" a captain would shout, and then get up himself to see that his order was obeyed. "Captain, take cover, sir!" the lieutenant-colonel would shriek, pacing up and down in the most exposed position that he could find.

O those cursed guns!—not the enemy's, but our own. Had it not been for them, we might have died like men. They must be supported, forsooth, the feeble, boasting bullies! It was impossible to conceive that these pieces were doing the enemy as excellent a mischief as his were doing us; they seemed to raise their "cloud by day" solely to direct aright the streaming procession of Confederate missiles. They no longer inspired confidence, but begot apprehension; and it was with grim satisfaction that I saw the carriage of one and another smashed into matchwood by a whooping shot and bundled out of the line.

X

The dense forests wholly or partly in which were fought so many battles of the Civil War, lay upon the earth in each autumn a thick deposit of dead leaves and stems, the decay of which forms a soil of surprising depth and richness. In dry weather the upper stratum is as inflammable as tinder. A fire once kindled in it will spread with a slow, persistent advance as far as local conditions permit, leaving a bed of light ashes beneath which the less combustible accretions of previous years will smolder until extinguished by rains. In many of the engagements of the war the fallen leaves took fire and roasted the fallen men. At Shiloh, during the first day's fighting, wide tracts of woodland were burned over in this way and scores of wounded who might have recovered perished in slow torture. I remember a deep ravine a little to the left and rear of the field I have described, in which, by some mad freak of heroic incompetence, a part of an Illinois regiment had been surrounded, and refusing to surrender was destroyed, as it very well deserved. My regiment having at last been relieved at the guns and moved over to the heights above this ravine for no obvious purpose, I obtained leave to go down into the valley of death and gratify a reprehensible curiosity.

Forbidding enough it was in every way. The fire had swept every superficial foot of it, and at every step I sank into ashes to the ankle. It had contained a thick undergrowth of young saplings, every one of which had been severed by a bullet, the foliage of the prostrate tops being afterward burnt and the stumps charred. Death had put his sickle into this thicket and fire had gleaned the field. Along a line which was not that of extreme depression, but was at every point significantly equidistant from the heights on either hand, lay the bodies half buried in ashes; some in the unlovely looseness of attitude denoting sudden death by the bullet, but by far the greater number in postures of agony that told of the tormenting flame. Their clothing was half burnt away—their hair and beard entirely; the rain had come too late to save their nails. Some were swollen to double girth; others shriveled to manikins. According to degree of exposure, their faces were bloated and black or yellow and shrunken. The contraction of muscles which had given them claws for hands had cursed each countenance with a hideous grin. Faugh! I cannot catalogue the charms of these gallant gentlemen who had got what they enlisted for.

XI

It was now three o'clock in the afternoon, and rain-
ing. For fifteen hours we had been wet to the skin.
Chilled, sleepy, hungry and disappointed—profoundly disgusted with the inglorious part to which
they had been condemned—the men of my regiment did everything doggedly. The spirit had gone
quite out of them. Blue sheets of powder smoke,
drifting amongst the trees, settling against the hill-
sides and beaten into nothingness by the falling rain,
filled the air with their peculiar pungent odor, but it
no longer stimulated. For miles on either hand could
be heard the hoarse murmur of the battle, breaking
out nearby with frightful distinctness, or sinking to a
murmur in the distance; and the one sound aroused
no more attention than the other.

We had been placed again in rear of those guns,
but even they and their iron antagonists seemed to
have tired of their feud, pounding away at one
another with amiable infrequency. The right of the
regiment extended a little beyond the field. On the
prolongation of the line in that direction were some
regiments of another division, with one in reserve. A
third of a mile back lay the remnant of somebody's
brigade looking to its wounds. The line of forest
bounding this end of the field stretched as straight as
a wall from the right of my regiment to Heaven
knows what regiment of the enemy. There suddenly

appeared, marching down along this wall, not more than two hundred yards in our front, a dozen files of gray-clad men with rifles on the right shoulder. At an interval of fifty yards they were followed by perhaps half as many more; and in fair supporting distance of these stalked with confident mien a single man! There seemed to me something indescribably ludicrous in the advance of this handful of men upon an army, albeit with their left flank protected by a forest. It does not so impress me now. They were the exposed flanks of three lines of infantry, each half a mile in length. In a moment our gunners had grappled with the nearest pieces, swung them half round, and were pouring streams of canister into the invaded wood. The infantry rose in masses, springing into line. Our threatened regiments stood like a wall, their loaded rifles at "ready," their bayonets hanging quietly in the scabbards. The right wing of my own regiment was thrown slightly backward to threaten the flank of the assault. The battered brigade away to the rear pulled itself together.

Then the storm burst. A great gray cloud seemed to spring out of the forest into the faces of the waiting battalions. It was received with a crash that made the very trees turn up their leaves. For one instant the assailants paused above their dead, then struggled forward, their bayonets glittering in the eyes that shone behind the smoke. One moment, and those unmoved men in blue would be impaled. What were they about? Why did they not fix bayonets? Were they stunned by their own volley? Their inaction was maddening! Another tremendous crash!—the rear rank had fired! Humanity, thank Heaven! is not made for this, and the shattered gray mass drew back a score of paces, opening a feeble fire. Lead had scored its old-time victory over steel; the heroic had broken its great heart against the commonplace. There are those who say that it is sometimes otherwise.

All this had taken but a minute of time, and now the second Confederate line swept down and poured in its fire. The line of blue staggered and gave way; in those two terrific volleys it seemed to have quite poured out its spirit. To this deadly work our reserve regiment now came up with a run. It was surprising to see it spitting fire with never a sound, for such was the infernal din that the ear could take in no more. This fearful scene was enacted within fifty paces of our toes, but we were rooted to the ground as if we had grown there. But now our commanding officer rode from behind us to the front, waved his hand with the courteous gesture that says *apres vous,* and with a barely audible cheer we sprang into the fight. Again the smoking front of gray receded, and again, as the enemy's third line emerged from its leafy covert, it pushed forward across the piles of dead and wounded to threaten with protruded steel. Never was seen so striking a proof of the paramount importance of numbers. Within an area of three hundred yards by fifty there struggled for front places no fewer than six regiments; and the accession of each, after the first collision, had it not been immediately counterpoised, would have turned the scale.

As matters stood, we were now very evenly matched, and how long we might have held out God only knows. But all at once something appeared to have gone wrong with the enemy's left; our men had somewhere pierced his line. A moment later his whole front gave way, and springing forward with fixed bayonets we pushed him in utter confusion back to his original line. Here, among the tents from which Grant's people had been expelled the day before, our broken and disordered regiments inextricably intermingled, and drunken with the wine of triumph, dashed confidently against a pair of trim battalions, provoking a tempest of hissing lead that made us stagger under its very weight. The sharp onset of another against our flank sent us whirling back with fire at our heels and fresh foes in merciless pursuit—who in their turn were broken upon the front of the invalided brigade previously mentioned, which had moved up from the rear to assist in this lively work.

As we rallied to reform behind our beloved guns and noted the ridiculous brevity of our line—as we sank from sheer fatigue, and tried to moderate the terrific thumping of our hearts—as we caught our

breath to ask who had seen such-and-such a comrade, and laughed hysterically at the reply—there
swept past us and over us into the open field a long
regiment with fixed bayonets and rifles on the right
shoulder. Another followed, and another; two—
three—four! Heavens! Where do all these men come
from, and why did they not come before? How
grandly and confidently they go sweeping on like
long blue waves of ocean chasing one another to the
cruel rocks! Involuntarily we draw in our weary feet
beneath us as we sit, ready to spring up and inter-
pose our breasts when these gallant lines shall come
back to us across the terrible field, and sift brokenly
through among the trees with spouting fires at their
backs. We still our breathing to catch the full grandeur
of the volleys that are to tear them to shreds. Minute
after minute passes and the sound does not come.
Then for the first time we note that the silence of
the whole region is not comparative, but absolute.
Have we become stone deaf? See; here comes a
stretcher-bearer, and there a surgeon! Good heavens!
a chaplain!

The battle was indeed at an end.

XII

And this was, O so long ago! How they come back
to me—dimly and brokenly, but with what a magic
spell—those years of youth when I was soldiering!
Again I hear the far warble of blown bugles. Again I

see the tall, blue smoke of camp-fires ascending from the dim valleys of Wonderland. There steals upon my sense the ghost of an odor from pines that canopy the ambuscade. I feel upon my cheek the morning mist that shrouds the hostile camp unaware of its doom, and my blood stirs at the ringing rifle-shot of the solitary sentinel. Unfamiliar landscapes, glittering with sunshine or sullen with rain, come to me demanding recognition, pass, vanish and give place to others. Here in the night stretches a wide and blasted field studded with half-extinct fires burning redly with I know not what presage of evil. Again I shudder as I note its desolation and its awful silence. Where was it? To what monstrous inharmony of death was it the visible prelude?

O days when all the world was beautiful and strange; when unfamiliar constellations burned in the Southern midnights, and the mocking-bird poured out his heart in the moon-gilded magnolia; when there was something new under a new sun; will your fine, far memories ever cease to lay contrasting pictures athwart the harsher features of this later world, accentuating the ugliness of the longer and tamer life? Is it not strange that the phantoms of a blood-stained period have so airy a grace and look with so tender eyes?—that I recall with difficulty the danger and death and horrors of the time, and without effort all that was gracious and picturesque?

Ah, Youth, there is no such wizard as thou! Give me but one touch of thine artist hand upon the dull canvas of the Present; gild for but one moment the drear and somber scenes of to-day, and I will willingly surrender another life than the one that I should have thrown away at Shiloh.

A Prisoner

[G. A. HENTY]

The party round the fire were just about to disperse when the captain of Vincent's troop approached. He took the horn of spirits and water that Vincent held up to him and tossed it off.

"That is a stirrup-cup, Wingfield."

"What! Are we for duty, captain?" Vincent asked as he rose to his feet.

"Yes; our troop and Harper's are to muster. Get the men together quietly. I think it is a serious business; each of the regiments furnish other troops, and I believe Stuart himself takes the command."

"That sounds like work, indeed," Vincent said. "I will get the troop together, sir."

"There are to be no trumpet calls, Wingfield; we are to get off as quietly as possible."

Most of the men were already fast asleep, but as soon as they learned that there was a prospect of active work all were full of life and animation. The girths of the saddles were tightened, swords buckled on, and revolvers carefully examined before being placed in the holsters. Many of the men carried repeating rifles, and the magazines were filled before these were slung across the riders' shoulders.

In a few minutes the three troops were mounted and in readiness for a start, and almost directly afterward Colonel Jones himself rode up and took the command. A thrill of satisfaction ran through the men as he did so, for it was certain that he would not himself be going in command of the detachment unless the occasion was an important one. For a few minutes no move was made.

"I suppose the others are going to join us here," Vincent said to the officer next to him.

"I suppose so," he replied. "We lie in the middle of the cavalry brigade with two regiments each side of us, so it is likely enough this is the gathering place. Yes, I can hear the tramping of horses."

"And I felt a spot of rain," Vincent said. "It has been lightning for some time. I fear we are in for a wet ride."

The contingent from the other regiments soon arrived, and just as the last came up General Stuart himself appeared and took his place at the head of the party, now some 500 strong. Short as the time had been since Vincent felt the first drop, the rain was now coming down in torrents. One by one the bright flames of the fires died down, and the darkness became so intense that Vincent could scarcely see the officer on his right hand.

"I hope the man who rode up with the general, and is no doubt to be our guide, knows the country well. It is no joke finding our way through a forest on such a night as this."

"I believe Stuart's got eyes like a cat," the officer said. "Sometimes on a dark night he has come galloping up to a post where I was in command, when one could scarcely see one's hand before one. It never seems to make any difference to him; day or night he rides about at a gallop."

"He trusts his horse," Vincent said. "That's the only way in the dark. They can see a lot better than we can, and if men would but let them go their own way instead of trying to guide them they would seldom run against anything. The only thing is to lie well down on the horse's neck; otherwise one might get swept out of the saddle by a bough. It's a question of nerve, I think not many of us would do as Stuart does, and trust himself entirely to his horse's instinct."

The word was now passed down the line that perfect silence was to be observed, and that they were to move forward in column, the ranks closing up as much as possible so as not to lose touch of each other. With heads bent down, and blankets wrapped round them as cloaks, the cavalry rode off through the pouring rain. The thunder was clashing over-head, and the flashes of the lightning enabled them to keep their places in close column. They went at a rapid trot, and even those who were ready to charge a body of the enemy, however numerous, without a moment's hesitation, experienced a feeling of nerv-ousness as they rode on in the darkness through the thick forest on their unknown errand. That they were going northward they knew, and knew also, after a short time, that they must be entering the lines of the enemy. They saw no signs of watch-fires, for these would long since have been quenched by the downpour. After half an hour's brisk riding all knew by the sharp sound of the beat of the horses' hoofs that they had left the soft track through the forest and were now upon a regular road.

"Thank goodness for that!" Vincent said in a low tone to his next neighbor. "I don't mind a brush with the enemy, but I own I don't like the idea that at any moment my brains may be knocked out by the branch of a tree."

"I quite agree with you," the other replied, "and I fancy every man felt the same."

There was no doubt as to this. Hitherto no sound had been heard save the jingling of accouterments and the dull heavy sound of the horses' tread; but now there could be heard mingled with these the buzz of voices, and occasionally a low laugh. They were so accustomed to wet that the soaking scarce inconvenienced them. They were out of the forest now, and felt sure of their guide; and as to the enemy, they only longed to discover them.

For another hour the rapid advance continued, and all felt sure that they must now have penetrated through the enemy's lines and be well in his rear. At last they heard a challenge of sentry. Then Stuart's voice shouted, "Charge!" and at full gallop they rode into the village at Catlet's Station on the Orange and Alexandria railroad, where General Pope had his headquarters. Another minute and they were in the midst of the enemy's camp, where the wildest confusion reigned. The Federal officers rushed from their tents and made off in the darkness; but the soldiers, who were lying on the line of railroad, leaped to their feet and opened a heavy fire upon their invisible foes. Against this the cavalry, broken up in the camp, with its tents, its animals, and its piles of baggage, could do little, for it was impossible to form them up in the broken and unknown ground.

The quarters of Pope were soon discovered; he himself had escaped, leaving his coat and hat behind. Many of his officers were captured, and in his quarters were found a box of official papers which were invaluable, as among them were copies of his letters asking for reinforcements, lists giving the strength and position of his troops, and other particulars of the greatest value to the Confederates. No time was lost, as the firing would set the whole Federal army on the alert, and they might find their retreat cut off. Therefore placing their prisoners in the center, and taking the box of papers with them, the cavalry were called off from the camp, and without delay started on their return ride.

They did not take the road by which they had come, but made a long detour, and just as daylight was breaking re-entered the Confederate lines without having encountered a foe from the time of their leaving Catlet's Station. Short as their stay in the camp had been, few of the men had returned empty-handed. The Northern army was supplied with an abundance of excellent food of all descriptions, forming the strongest possible contrast to the insufficient rations upon which the Confederate troops existed, and the troopers had helped themselves to whatever they could lay hands upon in the darkness and confusion.

Some rode in with a ham slung on each side of their saddle, others had secured a bottle or two of wine or spirits. Some had been fortunate enough to lay hands on some tins of coffee or a canister of tea, luxuries which for months had been unknown to them save when they were captured from the enemy. The only article captured of no possible utility was General Pope's coat, which was sent to Richmond, where it was hung up for public inspection; a wag sticking up a paper beside it, "This is the coat in which General Pope was going to ride in triumph into Richmond. The coat is here, but the general has not yet arrived."

The Confederates had lost but two or three men from the fire of the Federal infantry, and they were in high spirits at the success of their raid. No sooner had General Lee informed himself of the contents of the papers and the position of the enemy's forces than he determined to strike a heavy blow at him; and General Jackson, who had been sharply engaged with the enemy near Warrenton, was ordered to make a long detour, to cross the Blue Ridge mountains through Thoroughfare Gap, to fall upon Pope's rear and cut his communications with Washington, and if possible to destroy the vast depot of stores collected at Manassas.

The cavalry, under Stuart, were to accompany him. The march would be a tremendous one, the danger of thus venturing into the heart of the enemy's country immense, but the results of such an expedition would, if successful, be great; for Lee himself was to advance with his army on Pope's flank, and there was therefore a possibility of the utter defeat of that general before he could be joined by the army marching to reinforce him from Fredericksburg.

It was on Monday the 25th of August that Jackson started on his march, ascending the banks of the Rappahannock, and crossed the river at a ford, dragging his artillery with difficulty up the narrow and rocky road beyond. There was not a moment to be lost, for if the news reached the enemy the gorge known as Thoroughfare Gap would be occupied, and the whole object of the movement be defeated. Onward the force pushed, pressing on through fields and lanes without a single halt, until at night, hungry and weary but full of spirit, they marched into the little town of Salem, twenty miles from their starting-place. They had neither wagons nor provisions with them, and had nothing to eat but some ears of corn and green apples plucked on the road.

It was midnight when they reached Salem, and the inhabitants turned out in blank amazement at the sight of Confederate troops in that region, and welcomed the weary soldiers with the warmest manifestations. At daylight they were again upon the march, with Stuart's cavalry, as before, out upon each flank. Thoroughfare Gap was reached, and found undefended, and after thirty miles' marching the exhausted troops reached the neighborhood of Manassas. The men were faint from want of food, and many of them limped along barefooted; but they were full of enthusiasm.

Just at sunset, Stuart, riding on ahead, captured Bristoe, a station on the Orange and Alexandria Railroad four miles from Manassas. As they reached it a train came along at full speed. It was fired at, but did not stop, and got safely through to Manassas. Two trains that followed were captured; but by this time the alarm had spread, and no more trains arrived. Jackson had gained his point. He had placed himself on the line of communication of the enemy, but his position was a dangerous one indeed. Lee, who was following him, was still far away. An army was marching from Fredericksburg against him, another would be despatched from Washington as soon as the news of his presence was known, and Pope might turn and crush him before Lee could arrive to his assistance.

Worn out as the troops were, it was necessary at once to gain possession of Manassas, and the 21st North Carolina and 21st Georgia volunteered for the service, and, joined by Stuart with a portion of his cavalry, marched against it. After a brief contest the place was taken, the enemy stationed there being all taken prisoners. The amount of arms and stores captured was prodigious: Eight pieces of artillery, 250 horses, three locomotives, and tens of thousands of barrels of beef, pork, and flour, with an enormous quantity of public stores and the contents of innumerable sutlers' shops.

The sight of this vast abundance to starving men was tantalizing in the extreme. It was impossible to carry any of it away and all that could be done was to have at least one good meal. The troops therefore were marched in and each helped himself to as much as he could consume, and the ragged and barefooted men feasted upon tinned salmon and lobsters, champagne and dainties of every description forwarded for the use of officers. Then they set to work to pile the enormous mass of stores together and to set it on fire. While they were engaged at this a brigade of New Jersey troops which had come out from Washington to save Manassas was attacked and utterly routed. Ewell's division had remained at Bristoe, while those of Hill and Jackson moved to Manassas, and in the course of the afternoon Ewell saw the whole of Pope's army marching against him.

He held them in check for some hours, and thus gave the troops at Manassas time to destroy completely the vast accumulation of stores, and when Stuart's cavalry, covering the retreat, fell back at nightfall through Manassas, nothing but blackened cinders remained where the Federal depots had been situated. The blow to the Northerners was as heavy as it was unexpected. Pope had no longer either provisions for his men or forage for his cattle, and there was nothing left for him but to force his way past Jackson and retire upon Washington.

Jackson had now the option of falling back and allowing the enemy to pass, or of withstanding the whole Federal army with his own little force until Lee came up to the rescue. He chose the latter course, and took up a strong position. The sound of firing at Thoroughfare Gap was audible, and he knew that Longstreet's division of Lee's army was hotly engaged with a force which, now that it was too late, had been sent to hold the gorge. It was nearly sunset before Pope brought up his men to the attack. Jackson did not stand on the defensive, but rushed down and attacked the enemy—whose object had been to pass the position and press on— with such vigor that at nine o'clock they fell back.

An hour later a horseman rode up with the news that Longstreet had passed the Gap and was pressing on at full speed, and in the morning his forces were seen approaching, the line they were taking bringing them up at an angle to Jackson's position. Thus their formation as they arrived was that of an open V, and it was through the angle of this V that Pope had to force his way. Before Longstreet could arrive, however, the enemy hurled themselves upon Jackson, and for hours the Confederates held their own against the vast Federal army, Longstreet's force being too far away to lend them a hand. Ammunition failed, and the soldiers fought with piles of stones, but night fell without any impression being made upon these veterans. General Lee now came up with General Hood's division, and hurled this against the Federals and drove them back. In the evening Longstreet's force took up the position General Lee had assigned to it, and in the morning all the Confederate army had arrived, and the battle recommenced.

The struggle was long and terrible; but by nightfall every attack had been repulsed, and the Confederates, advancing on all sides, drove the Northerners, a broken and confused crowd, before them, the darkness alone saving them from utter destruction. Had there been but one hour more of daylight the defeat would have been as complete as was that in the battle of Bull Run, which had been fought on precisely the same ground. However, under cover of the darkness the Federals retreated to Centreville, whence they were driven on the following day.

In the tremendous fighting in which Jackson's command had for three long days been engaged, the cavalry bore a comparatively small part. The Federal artillery was too powerful to permit the employment of large bodies of cavalry and although from time to time charges were made when an opportunity seemed to offer itself, the battle was fought out by the infantry and artillery. When the end came Jackson's command was for a time *hors de combat*. During the long two days' march they had at least gathered corn and apples to sustain life; but during these three days' fighting they had had no food whatever, and many were so weak that they could no longer march.

They had done all that was possible for men to do; had for two days withstood the attack of an enemy of five times their numbers, and had on the final day borne their full share in the great struggle, but now the greater part could do no more, thousands of men were unable to drag themselves a step further, and

Lee's army was reduced in strength for the time by nearly 20,000 men. All these afterward rejoined it; some as soon as they recovered limped away to take their places in the ranks again, others made their way to the depot at Warrenton, where Lee had ordered that all unable to accompany his force should rendezvous until he returned and they were able to rejoin their regiments.

Jackson marched away and laid siege to Harper's Ferry, an important depot garrisoned by 11,000 men, who were forced to surrender just as McClellan with a fresh army, 100,000 strong, which was pressing forward to its succor, arrived within a day's march. As soon as Jackson had taken the place he hurried away with his troops to join Lee, who was facing the enemy at the Antietam river. Here upon the following day another terrible battle was fought; the Confederates, though but 39,000 strong, repulsing every attack by the Federals, and driving them with terrible slaughter back across the river.

Their own loss, however, had been very heavy, and Lee, knowing that he could expect no assistance, while the enemy were constantly receiving reinforcements, waited for a day to collect his wounded, bury his dead, and send his stores and artillery to the rear, and then retired unpursued across the Rappahannock. Thus the hard-fought campaign came to an end.

Vincent Wingfield was not with the army that retired across the Rappahannock. A portion of the cavalry had followed the broken Federals to the very edge of the stream, and just as they reined in their horses a round shot from one of the Federal batteries carried away his cap, and he fell as if dead from his horse. During the night some of the Northerners crossed the stream to collect and bring back their own wounded who had fallen near it, and coming across Vincent, and finding that he still breathed, and was apparently without a wound, they carried him back with them across the river as a prisoner.

Vincent had indeed escaped without a wound, having been only stunned by the passage of the shot that had carried away his cap, and missed him but by the fraction of an inch. He had begun to recover consciousness just as his captors came up, and the action of carrying him completely restored him. That he had fallen into the hands of the Northerners he was well aware; but he was unable to imagine how this had happened. He remembered that the Confederates had been, up to the moment when he fell, completely successful, and he could only imagine that in a subsequent attack the Federals had turned the tables upon them.

How he himself had fallen, or what had happened to him, he had no idea. Beyond a strange feeling of numbness in the head he was conscious of no injury, and he could only imagine that his horse had been shot under him, and that he must have fallen upon his head. The thought that his favorite horse was killed afflicted him almost as much as his own capture. As soon as his captors perceived that their prisoner's consciousness had returned they at once reported that an officer of Stuart's cavalry had been taken, and at daybreak next morning General McClellan on rising was acquainted with the fact, and Vincent was conducted to his tent.

"You are unwounded, sir?" the general said in some surprise.

"I am, general," Vincent replied. "I do not know how it happened, but I believe that my horse must have been shot under me, and that I must have been thrown and stunned; however, I remember nothing from the moment when I heard the word halt, just as we reached the side of the stream, to that when I found myself being carried here."

"You belong to the cavalry?"

"Yes, sir."

"Was Lee's force all engaged yesterday?"

"I do not know," Vincent said. "I only came up with Jackson's division from Harper's Ferry the evening before."

"I need not have questioned you," McClellan said. "I know that Lee's whole army, 100,000 strong, opposed me yesterday."

Vincent was silent. He was glad to see that the Federal general, as usual, enormously overrated the strength of the force opposed to him.

"I hear that the whole of the garrison of Harper's Ferry were released on parole not to serve again during the war. If you are ready to give me your promise to the same effect I will allow you to return to your friends; if not, you must remain a prisoner until you are regularly exchanged."

"I must do so, then, general," Vincent said quietly. "I could not return home and remain inactive while every man in the South is fighting for the defense of his country, so I will take my chance of being exchanged."

"I am sorry you choose that alternative," McClellan said. "I hate to see brave men imprisoned if only for a day; and braver men than those across yonder stream are not to be found. My officers and men are astonished. They seem so thin and worn as to be scarce able to lift a musket, their clothes are fit only for a scarecrow, they are indeed pitiful objects to look at; but the way in which they fight is wonderful. I could not have believed had I not seen it, that men could have charged as they did again and again across ground swept by a tremendous artillery and musketry fire; it was wonderful! I can tell you, young sir, that even though you beat us we are proud of you as our countrymen; and I believe that if your General Jackson were to ride through our camp he would be cheered as lustily and heartily by our men as he is by his own."

Some fifty or sixty other prisoners had been taken; they had been captured in the hand-to-hand struggle that had taken place on some parts of the field, having got separated from their corps and mixed up with the enemy, and carried off the field with them as they retired. These for the most part accepted the offered parole; but some fifteen, like Vincent, preferred a Northern prison to promising to abstain from fighting in defense of their country, and in the middle of the day they were placed together in a tent under a guard at the rear of the camp.

The next morning came the news that Lee had fallen back. There was exultation among the Federals, not unmingled with a strong sense of relief; for the heavy losses inflicted in the previous fighting had taken all the ardor of attack out of McClellan's army, and they were glad indeed that they were not to be called upon to make another attempt to drive the Confederates from their position. Vincent was no less pleased at the news. He knew how thin were the ranks of the Confederate fighting men, and how greatly they were worn and exhausted by fatigue and want of food, and that, although they had the day before repulsed the attacks of the masses of well-fed Northerners, such tremendous exertions could not often be repeated, and a defeat, with the river in their rear, approachable only by one rough and narrow road, would have meant a total destruction of the army.

The next morning Vincent and his companions
were put into the train and sent to Alexandria. They
had no reason to complain of their treatment upon
the way. They were well fed, and after their starvation diet for the last six weeks their rations seemed
to them actually luxurious. The Federal troops in
Alexandria, who were for the most part young
recruits who had just arrived from the north and
west, looked with astonishment upon these thin and
ragged men, several of whom were barefooted. Was it
possible that such scarecrows as these could in every
battle have driven back the well-fed and cared-for
Northern soldiers!

"Are they all like this?" one burly young soldier
from a western state asked their guard.

"That's them, sir," the sergeant in charge of the
party replied. "Not much to look at, are they? But,
by gosh, you should see them fight! You wouldn't
think of their looks then."

"If that's soldiering," the young farmer said
solemnly, "the sooner I am back home again the better. But it don't seem to me altogether strange as
they should fight so hard, because I should say they
must look upon it as a comfort to be killed rather
than to live like that."

A shout of laughter from the prisoners showed the
young rustic that the objects of his pity did not consider life to be altogether intolerable even under
such circumstances, and he moved away meditating

on the discomforts of war, and upon the remarks that would be made were he to return home in so sorrowful a plight as that of these Confederate prisoners.

"I bargained to fight," he said, "and though I don't expect I shall like it, I sha'n't draw back when the time comes; but as to being starved till you are nigh a skeleton, and going about barefooted and in such rags as a tramp wouldn't look at, it ain't reasonable." And yet, had he known it, among those fifteen prisoners more than half were possessors of wide estates, and had been brought up from their childhood in the midst of luxuries such as the young farmer never dreamed of.

Among many of the soldiers sympathy took a more active form, and men pressed forward and gave packets of tobacco, cigars, and other little presents to them, while two or three pressed rolls of dollar notes into their hands, with words of rough kindness.

"There ain't no ill feeling in us, Rebs. You have done your work like men and no doubt you thinks your cause is right, just as we does; but it's all over now, and maybe our turn will come next to see the inside of one of your prisons down south. So we are just soldiers together, and can feel for each other."

Discipline in small matters was never strictly enforced in the American armies, and the sergeant in charge offered no opposition to the soldiers mingling with the prisoners as they walked along.

Two days later they were sent by railway to the great prison at Elmira, a town in the southwest of the State of New York. When they reached the jail the prisoners were separated; Vincent, who was the only officer, being assigned quarters with some twenty others of the same rank. The prisoners crowded round him as he entered, eager to hear the last news from the front, for they heard from their guards only news of constant victories won by the Northerners; for every defeat was transformed by the Northern papers into a brilliant victory, and it was only when the shattered remains of the various armies returned to Alexandria to be re-formed that the truth gradually leaked out. Thus Antietam had been claimed as a great Northern victory, for although McClellan's troops had in the battle been hurled back shattered and broken across the river, two days afterward Lee had retired.

One of the prisoners, who was also dressed in cavalry uniform, hung back from the rest, and going to the window looked out while Vincent was chatting with the others. Presently he turned round, and Vincent recognized with surprise his old opponent Jackson. After a moment's hesitation he walked across the room to him.

"Jackson," he said, "we have not been friends lately, but I don't see why we should keep up our quarrel any longer; we got on all right at school together; and now that we are prisoners together here it would be foolish to continue our quarrel. Perhaps we were both somewhat to blame in that affair. I am quite willing to allow I was, for one, but I think we might well put it all aside now."

Jackson hesitated, and then took the hand Vincent held out to him.

"That's right, young fellows," one of the other officers said. "Now that every Southern gentleman is fighting and giving his life, if need be, for his country, no one has a right to have private quarrels of his own. Life is short enough as it is, certainly too short to indulge in private animosities. A few weeks ago we were fighting side by side, and facing death together; to-day we are prisoners; a week hence we may be exchanged, and soon take our places in the ranks again. It's the duty of all Southerners to stand shoulder to shoulder, and there ought to be no such thing as ill-feeling among ourselves."

Vincent was not previously aware that Jackson had obtained a commission. He now learned that he had been chosen by his comrades to fill a vacancy caused by the death of an officer in a skirmish just before Pope fell back from the Rappahannock, and that he had been made prisoner a few days afterward in a charge against a greatly superior body of Federal cavalry.

The great majority of the officers on both sides were at the commencement of the war chosen by their comrades, the elections at first taking place once a year. This, however, was found to act very badly. In some cases the best men in the regiment were chosen; but too often men who had the command of money, and could afford to stand treat and get in supplies of food and spirits, were elected. The evils of the system were found so great, indeed, that it was gradually abandoned; but in cases of vacancies occurring in the field, and there being a necessity for at once filling them up, the colonels of the regiments had power to make appointments, and if the choice of the men was considered to be satisfactory their nominee would be generally chosen.

In the case of Jackson, the colonel had hesitated in confirming the choice of the men. He did not for a moment suspect him to be wanting in courage; but he regarded him as one who shirked his work, and who won the votes of the men rather by a fluent tongue and by the violence of his expressions of hatred against the North than by any soldierly qualities.

Some of the officers had been months in prison, and they were highly indignant at the delays that had occurred in effecting their exchange. The South, indeed, would have been only too glad to get rid of some of their numerous prisoners, who were simply an expense and trouble to them, and to get their own men back into their ranks. They could ill spare the soldiers required to guard so large a number of prisoners, and a supply of food was in itself a serious matter.

Thus it was that at Harper's Ferry and upon a good many other occasions they released vast numbers of prisoners on their simple paroles not to serve again. The North, however, were in no hurry to make exchange; and moreover, their hands were so full with their enormous preparations that they put aside all matters which had not the claim of urgency.

A Night

[**LOUISA MAY ALCOTT**]

Being fond of the night side of nature, I was soon promoted to the post of night nurse, with every facility for indulging in my favorite pastime of "owling." My colleague, a black-eyed widow, relieved me at dawn, we two taking care of the ward, between us, like the immortal Sairy and Betsey, "turn and turn about." I usually found my boys in the jolliest state of mind their condition allowed; for it was a known fact that Nurse Periwinkle objected to blue devils, and entertained a belief that he who laughed most was surest of recovery. At the beginning of my reign, dumps and dismals prevailed; the nurses looked anxious and tired, the men gloomy or sad; and a general "Hark!-from-the-tombs-a-doleful-sound" style of conversation seemed to be the fashion: a state of things which caused one coming from a merry, social New England town, to feel as if she had got into an exhausted receiver; and the instinct of self-preservation, to say nothing of a philanthropic desire to serve the race, caused a speedy change in Ward No. 1.

More flattering than the most gracefully turned compliment, more grateful than the most admiring glance, was the sight of those rows of faces, all strange to me a little while ago, now lighting up, with smiles of welcome, as I came among them, enjoying that moment heartily, with a womanly pride in their regard, a motherly affection for them all. The evenings were spent in reading aloud, writing letters, waiting on and amusing the men, going the rounds with Dr. P., as he made his second daily survey, dressing my dozen wounds afresh, giving last doses, and making them cozy for the long hours to come, till the nine o'clock bell rang, the gas was turned down, the day nurses went off duty, the night watch came on, and my nocturnal adventure began.

My ward was now divided into three rooms; and, under favor of the matron, I had managed to sort out the patients in such a way that I had what I called, "my duty room," my "pleasure room," and my "pathetic room," and worked for each in a different way. One, I visited, armed with a dressing tray, full of rollers, plasters, and pins; another, with books, flowers, games, and gossip; a third, with teapots, lullabies, consolation, and sometimes, a shroud.

Wherever the sickest or most helpless man chanced to be, there I held my watch, often visiting the other rooms, to see that the general watchman of the ward did his duty by the fires and the wounds, the latter needing constant wetting. Not only on this account did I meander, but also to get fresher air than the close rooms afforded; for, owing to the stupidity of that mysterious "somebody" who does all the damage in the world, the windows had been carefully nailed down above, and the lower sashes could only be raised in the mildest weather, for the men lay just below. I had suggested a summary smashing of a few panes here and there, when frequent appeals to headquarters had proved unavailing, and daily orders to lazy attendants had come to nothing. No one seconded the motion, however, and the nails were far beyond my reach; for, though belonging to the sisterhood of "ministering angels," I had no wings, and might as well have asked for Jacob's ladder, as a pair of steps, in that charitable chaos.

One of the harmless ghosts who bore me company during the haunted hours, was Dan, the watchman, whom I regarded with a certain awe; for, though so much together, I never fairly saw his face, and, but for his legs, should never have recognized him, as we seldom met by day. These legs were remarkable, as was his whole figure, for his body was short, rotund, and done up in a big jacket, and muffler; his beard hid the lower part of his face, his hat-brim the upper; and all I ever discovered was a pair of sleepy eyes, and a very mild voice. But the legs!—very long, very thin, very crooked and feeble, looking like gray sausages in their tight coverings, without a ray of pegtopishness about them, and finished off with a pair of expansive, green cloth shoes, very like Chinese junks, with the sails down. This figure, gliding noiselessly about the dimly lighted rooms, was strongly suggestive of the spirit of a beer barrel mounted on corkscrews, haunting the old hotel in search of its lost mates, emptied and staved in long ago.

Another goblin who frequently appeared to me, was the attendant of the pathetic room, who, being a faithful soul, was often up to tend two or three men, weak and wandering as babies, after the fever had gone. The amiable creature beguiled the watches of the night by brewing jorums of a fearful beverage, which he called coffee, and insisted on sharing with me; coming in with a great bowl of something like mud soup, scalding hot, guiltless of cream, rich in an all-pervading flavor of molasses, scorch and tin pot. Such an amount of good will and neighborly kindness also went into the mess, that I never could find the heart to refuse, but always received it with thanks, sipped it with hypocritical relish while he remained, and whipped it into the slop-jar the instant he departed, thereby gratifying him, securing one rousing laugh in the doziest hour of the night, and no one was the worse for the transaction but the pigs. Whether they were "cut off untimely in their sins," or not, I carefully abstained from inquiring.

It was a strange life—asleep half the day, exploring Washington the other half, and all night hovering, like a massive cherubim, in a red rigolette, over the slumbering sons of man. I liked it, and found many things to amuse, instruct, and interest me. The snores alone were quite a study, varying from the mild sniff to the stentorian snort, which startled the echoes and hoisted the performer erect to accuse his neighbor of the deed, magnanimously forgive him, and wrapping the drapery of his couch about him, lie down to vocal slumber. After listening for a week to this band of wind instruments, I indulged in the belief that I could recognize each by the snore alone, and was tempted to join the chorus by breaking out with John Brown's favorite hymn:

"Blow ye the trumpet, blow!"

I would have given much to have possessed the art of sketching, for many of the faces became wonderfully interesting when unconscious. Some grew stern and grim, the men evidently dreaming of war, as they gave orders, groaned over their wounds, or damned the rebels vigorously; some grew sad and infinitely pathetic, as if the pain borne silently all day, revenged itself by now betraying what the man's pride had concealed so well. Often the roughest grew young and pleasant when sleep smoothed the hard lines away, letting the real nature assert itself;

many almost seemed to speak, and I learned to know these men better by night than through any intercourse by day. Sometimes they disappointed me, for faces that looked merry and good in the light, grew bad and sly when the shadows came; and though they made no confidences in words, I read their lives, leaving them to wonder at the change of manner this midnight magic wrought in their nurse. A few talked busily; one drummer boy sang sweetly, though no persuasions could win a note from him by day; and several depended on being told what they had talked of in the morning.

Even my constitutionals in the chilly halls, possessed a certain charm, for the house was never still. Sentinels tramped round it all night long, their muskets glittering in the wintry moonlight as they walked, or stood before the doors, straight and silent, as figures of stone, causing one to conjure up romantic visions of guarded forts, sudden surprises, and daring deeds; for in these war times the hum drum life of Yankeedom had vanished, and the most prosaic feel some thrill of that excitement which stirs the nation's heart, and makes its capital a camp of hospitals.

Wandering up and down these lower halls, I often heard cries from above, steps hurrying to and fro, saw surgeons passing up, or men coming down carrying a stretcher, where lay a long white figure, whose face was shrouded and whose fight was done. Sometimes I stopped to watch the passers in the street, the moonlight shining on the spire opposite, or the gleam of some vessel floating, like a white-winged sea-gull, down the broad Potomac, whose fullest flow can never wash away the red stain of the land.

The night whose events I have a fancy to record, opened with a little comedy, and closed with a great tragedy; for a virtuous and useful life untimely ended is always tragical to those who see not as God sees. My headquarters were beside the bed of a New Jersey boy, crazed by the horrors of that dreadful Saturday. A slight wound in the knee brought him there; but his mind had suffered more than his body; some string of that delicate machine was over strained, and, for days, he had been reliving in imagination, the scenes he could not forget, till his distress broke out in incoherent ravings, pitiful to hear. As I sat by him, endeavoring to soothe his poor distracted brain by the constant touch of wet hands over his hot forehead, he lay cheering his comrades on, hurrying them back, then counting them as they fell around him, often clutching my arm, to drag me from the vicinity of a bursting shell, or covering up his head to screen himself from a shower of shot; his face brilliant with fever; his eyes restless; his head never still; every muscle strained and rigid; while an incessant stream of defiant shouts, whispered warnings, and broken laments, poured from his lips with that forceful bewilderment which makes such wanderings so hard to overhear.

It was past eleven, and my patient was slowly wearying himself into fitful intervals of quietude, when, in one of these pauses, a curious sound arrested my attention. Looking over my shoulder, I saw a one-legged phantom hopping nimbly down the room; and, going to meet it, recognized a certain Pennsylvania gentleman, whose wound-fever had taken a turn for the worse, and, depriving him of the few wits a drunken campaign had left him, set him literally tripping on the light, fantastic toe "toward home," as he blandly informed me, touching the military cap which formed a striking contrast to the severe simplicity of the rest of his decidedly undress uniform. When sane, the least movement produced a roar of pain or a volley of oaths; but the departure of reason seemed to have wrought an agreeable change, both in the man and his manners; for, balancing himself on one leg, like a meditative stork, he plunged into an animated discussion of the war, the President, lager beer, and Enfield rifles, regardless of any suggestions of mine as to the propriety of returning to bed, lest he be court-martialed for desertion.

Anything more supremely ridiculous can hardly be imagined than this figure, scantily draped in white, its one foot covered with a big blue sock, a dingy cap set rakingly askew on its shaven head, and placid satisfaction beaming in its broad red face, as it flourished a mug in one hand, an old boot in the other, calling them canteen and knapsack, while it skipped and fluttered in the most unearthly fashion. What to do with the creature I didn't know; Dan was absent, and if I went to find him, the perambulator might festoon himself out of the window, set his toga on fire, or do some of his neighbors a mischief. The attendant of the room was sleeping like a near relative of the celebrated Seven, and nothing short of pins would rouse him; for he had been out that day, and whiskey asserted its supremacy in balmy whiffs. Still declaiming, in a fine flow of eloquence, the demented gentleman hopped on, blind and deaf to my graspings and entreaties; and I was about to slam the door in his face, and run for help, when a second and saner phantom, "all in white," came to the rescue, in the likeness of a big Prussian, who spoke no English, but divined the crisis, and put an end to it, by bundling the lively monoped into his bed, like a baby, with an authoritative command to "stay put," which received added weight from being delivered in an odd conglomeration of French and German, accompanied by warning wags of a head decorated with a yellow cotton night cap, rendered most imposing by a tassel like a bell-pull. Rather exhausted by his excursion, the member from Pennsylvania subsided; and, after an irrepressible laugh together, my Prussian ally and myself were returning to our places, when the echo of a sob caused us to glance along the beds. It came from one in the corner—such a little bed!—and such a tearful little face looked up at us, as we stopped beside it! The twelve-year-old drummer boy was not singing now, but sobbing, with a manly effort all the while to stifle the distressful sounds that would break out.

"What is it, Teddy?" I asked, as he rubbed the tears away, and checked himself in the middle of a great sob to answer plaintively:

"I've got a chill, ma'am, but I ain't cryin' for that, 'cause I'm used to it. I dreamed Kit was here, and when I waked up he wasn't, and I couldn't help it, then."

The boy came in with the rest, and the man who was taken dead from the ambulance was the Kit he mourned. Well he might; for, when the wounded were brought from Fredericksburg, the child lay in one of the camps thereabout, and this good friend, though sorely hurt himself, would not leave him to the exposure and neglect of such a time and place; but, wrapping him in his own blanket, carried him in his arms to the transport, tended him during the passage, and only yielded up his charge when Death met him at the door of the hospital which promised care and comfort for the boy. For ten days, Teddy had shivered or burned with fever and ague, pining the while for Kit, and refusing to be comforted, because he had not been able to thank him for the generous protection, which, perhaps, had cost the giver's life. The vivid dream had wrung the childish heart with a fresh pang, and when I tried the solace fitted for his years, the remorseful fear that haunted him found vent in a fresh burst of tears, as he looked at the wasted hands I was endeavoring to warm:

"Oh! if I'd only been as thin when Kit carried me as I am now, maybe he wouldn't have died; but I was heavy, he was hurt worser than we knew, and so it killed him; and I didn't see him, to say good bye."

This thought had troubled him in secret; and my assurances that his friend would probably have died at all events, hardly assuaged the bitterness of his regretful grief.

At this juncture, the delirious man began to shout; the one-legged rose up in his bed, as if preparing for another dart, Teddy bewailed himself more piteously than before: and if ever a woman was at her wit's end, that distracted female was Nurse Periwinkle, during the space of two or three minutes, as she vibrated between the three beds, like an agitated pendulum. Like a most opportune reinforcement, Dan, the bandy, appeared, and devoted himself to the lively party, leaving me free to return to my post; for the Prussian, with a nod and a smile, took the lad away to his own bed, and lulled him to sleep with a soothing murmur, like a mammoth humblebee. I liked that in Fritz, and if he ever wondered afterward at the dainties that sometimes found their way into his rations, or the extra comforts of his bed, he might have found a solution of the mystery in sundry persons' knowledge of the fatherly action of that night.

Hardly was I settled again, when the inevitable bowl appeared, and its bearer delivered a message I had expected, yet dreaded to receive:

"John is going, ma'am, and wants to see you, if you can come."

"The moment this boy is asleep; tell him so, and let me know if I am in danger of being too late."

My Ganymede departed, and while I quieted poor Shaw, I thought of John. He came in a day or two after the others; and, one evening, when I entered my "pathetic room," I found a lately emptied bed occupied by a large, fair man, with a fine face, and the serenest eyes I ever met. One of the earlier comers had often spoken of a friend, who had remained behind, that those apparently worse wounded than himself might reach a shelter first. It seemed a David and Jonathan sort of friendship. The man fretted for his mate, and was never tired of praising John—his courage, sobriety, self-denial, and unfailing kindliness of heart; always winding up with: "He's an out an' out fine feller, ma'am; you see if he ain't."

I had some curiosity to behold this piece of excellence, and when he came, watched him for a night or two, before I made friends with him; for, to tell the truth, I was a little afraid of the stately looking man, whose bed had to be lengthened to accommodate his commanding stature; who seldom spoke, uttered no complaint, asked no sympathy, but tranquilly observed what went on about him; and, as he lay high upon his pillows, no picture of dying statesman or warrior was ever fuller of real dignity than this Virginia blacksmith. A most attractive face he had, framed in brown hair and beard, comely featured and full of vigor, as yet unsubdued by pain; thoughtful and often beautifully mild while watching the afflictions of others, as if entirely forgetful of his own. His mouth was grave and firm, with plenty of will and courage in its lines, but a smile could make it as sweet as any woman's; and his eyes were child's eyes, looking one fairly in the face, with a clear, straightforward glance, which promised well for such as placed their faith in him. He seemed to cling to life, as if it were rich in duties and delights, and he had learned the secret of content. The only time I saw his composure disturbed, was when my surgeon brought another to examine John, who scrutinized their faces with an anxious look, asking of the elder: "Do you think I shall pull through, sir?" "I hope so, my man." And, as the two passed on, John's eye still followed them, with an intentness which would have won a clearer answer from them, had they seen it. A momentary shadow flitted over his face; then came the usual serenity, as if, in that brief eclipse, he had acknowledged the existence of some hard possibility, and, asking nothing yet hoping all things, left the issue in God's hands, with that submission which is true piety.

The next night, as I went my rounds with Dr. P., I happened to ask which man in the room probably suffered most; and, to my great surprise, he glanced at John:

"Every breath he draws is like a stab; for the ball pierced the left lung, broke a rib, and did no end of damage here and there; so the poor lad can find neither forgetfulness nor ease, because he must lie on his wounded back or suffocate. It will be a hard struggle, and a long one, for he possesses great vitality; but even his temperate life can't save him; I wish it could."

"You don't mean he must die, Doctor?"

"Bless you there's not the slightest hope for him; and you'd better tell him so before long; women have a way of doing such things comfortably, so I leave it to you. He won't last more than a day or two, at furthest."

I could have sat down on the spot and cried heartily, if I had not learned the wisdom of bottling up one's tears for leisure moments. Such an end seemed very hard for such a man, when half a dozen worn out, worthless bodies round him, were gathering up the remnants of wasted lives, to linger on for years perhaps, burdens to others, daily reproaches to themselves. The army needed men like John, earnest, brave, and faithful; fighting for liberty and justice with both heart and hand, true soldiers of the Lord. I could not give him up so soon, or think with any patience of so excellent a nature robbed of its fulfillment, and blundered into eternity by the rashness or stupidity of those at whose hands so many lives may be required. It was an easy thing for Dr. P. to say: "Tell him he must die," but a cruelly hard thing to do, and by no means as "comfortable" as he politely suggested. I had not the heart to do it then, and privately indulged the hope that some change for the better might take place, in spite of gloomy prophesies; so, rendering my task unnecessary. A few minutes later, as I came in again, with fresh rollers, I saw John sitting erect, with no one to support him, while the surgeon dressed his back. I had never hitherto seen it done; for, having simpler wounds to attend to, and knowing the fidelity of the attendant, I had left John to him, thinking it might be more agreeable and safe; for both strength and experience were needed in his case. I had forgotten that the strong man might long for the gentle tendance of a woman's hands, the sympathetic magnetism of a woman's presence, as well as the feebler souls about him. The Doctor's words caused me to reproach myself with neglect, not of any real duty perhaps, but of those little cares and kindnesses that solace homesick spirits, and make the heavy hours pass easier. John looked lonely and forsaken just then, as he sat with bent head, hands folded on his knee, and no outward sign of suffering, till, looking nearer, I saw great tears roll down and drop upon the floor. It was a new sight there; for, though I had seen many suffer, some swore, some groaned, most endured silently, but none wept. Yet it did not seem weak, only very touching, and straightway my fear vanished, my heart opened wide and took him in, as, gathering the bent head in my arms, as freely as if he had been a little child, I said, "Let me help you bear it, John."

Never, on any human countenance, have I seen so swift and beautiful a look of gratitude, surprise and comfort, as that which answered me more eloquently than the whispered—

"Thank you, ma'am, this is right good! This is what I wanted!"

"Then why not ask for it before?"

"I didn't like to be a trouble; you seemed so busy, and I could manage to get on alone."

"You shall not want it any more, John."

Nor did he; for now I understood the wistful look that sometimes followed me, as I went out, after a brief pause beside his bed, or merely a passing nod, while busied with those who seemed to need me more than he, because more urgent in their demands; now I knew that to him, as to so many, I was the poor substitute for mother, wife, or sister, and in his eyes no stranger, but a friend who hitherto had seemed neglectful; for, in his modesty, he had never guessed the truth. This was changed now; and, through the tedious operation of probing, bathing, and dressing his wounds, he leaned against me, holding my hand fast, and, if pain wrung further tears from him, no one saw them fall but me. When he was laid down again, I hovered about him, in a remorseful state of mind that would not let me rest, till I had bathed his face, brushed his "bonny brown hair," set all things smooth about him, and laid a knot of heath and heliotrope on his clean pillow. While doing this, he watched me with the satisfied expression I so liked to see; and when I offered the little nosegay, held it carefully in his great hand, smoothed a ruffled leaf or two, surveyed and smelt it with an air of genuine delight, and lay contentedly regarding the glimmer of the sunshine on the green. Although the manliest man among my forty, he said, "Yes, ma'am," like a little boy; received suggestions for his comfort with the quick smile that brightened his whole face; and now and then, as I stood tidying the table by his bed, I felt him softly touch my gown, as if to assure himself that I was there. Anything more natural and frank I never saw, and found this brave John as bashful as brave, yet full of excellencies and fine aspirations, which, having no power to express themselves in words, seemed to have bloomed into his character and made him what he was.

After that night, an hour of each evening that remained to him was devoted to his ease or pleasure. He could not talk much, for breath was precious, and he spoke in whispers; but from occasional conversations, I gleaned scraps of private history which only added to the affection and respect I felt for him. Once he asked me to write a letter, and as I settled pen and paper, I said, with an irrepressible glimmer of feminine curiosity, "Shall it be addressed to wife, or mother, John?"

"Neither, ma'am; I've got no wife, and will write to mother myself when I get better. Did you think I was married because of this?" he asked, touching a plain ring he wore, and often turned thoughtfully on his finger when he lay alone.

"Partly that, but more from a settled sort of look you have; a look which young men seldom get until they marry."

"I didn't know that; but I'm not so very young, ma'am, thirty in May, and have been what you might call settled this ten years; for mother's a widow, I'm the oldest child she has, and it wouldn't do for me to marry until Lizzy has a home of her own, and Laurie's learned his trade; for we're not rich, and I must be father to the children and husband to the dear old woman, if I can."

"No doubt but you are both, John; yet how came you to go to war, if you felt so? Wasn't enlisting as bad as marrying?"

"No, ma'am, not as I see it, for one is helping my neighbor, the other pleasing myself. I went because I couldn't help it. I didn't want the glory or the pay; I wanted the right thing done, and people kept saying the men who were in earnest ought to fight. I was in earnest, the Lord knows! But I held off as long as I could, not knowing which was my duty; mother saw the case, gave me her ring to keep me steady, and said 'Go:' so I went."

A short story and a simple one, but the man and the mother were portrayed better than pages of fine writing could have done it.

"Do you ever regret that you came, when you lie here suffering so much?"

"Never, ma'am; I haven't helped a great deal, but I've shown I was willing to give my life, and perhaps I've got to; but I don't blame anybody, and if it was to do over again, I'd do it. I'm a little sorry I wasn't wounded in front; it looks cowardly to be hit in the back, but I obeyed orders, and it don't matter in the end, I know."

Poor John! It did not matter now, except that a shot in the front might have spared the long agony in store for him. He seemed to read the thought that troubled me, as he spoke so hopefully when there was no hope, for he suddenly added:

"This is my first battle; do they think it's going to be my last?"

"I'm afraid they do, John."

It was the hardest question I had ever been called upon to answer; doubly hard with those clear eyes fixed on mine, forcing a truthful answer by their own truth. He seemed a little startled at first, pondered over the fateful fact a moment, then shook his head, with a glance at the broad chest and muscular limbs stretched out before him:

"I'm not afraid, but it's difficult to believe all at once. I'm so strong it don't seem possible for such a little wound to kill me."

Merry Mercutio's dying words glanced through my memory as he spoke: "'Tis not so deep as a well, nor so wide as a church door, but 'tis enough." And John would have said the same could he have seen the ominous black holes between his shoulders; he never had; and, seeing the ghastly sights about him, could not believe his own wound more fatal than these, for all the suffering it caused him.

"Shall I write to your mother, now?" I asked, thinking that these sudden tidings might change all plans and purposes; but they did not; for the man received the order of the Divine Commander to march with the same unquestioning obedience with which the soldier had received that of the human one; doubtless remembering that the first led him to life, and the last to death.

"No, ma'am; to Laurie just the same; he'll break it to her best, and I'll add a line to her myself when you get done."

So I wrote the letter which he dictated, finding it better than any I had sent; for, though here and there a little ungrammatical or inelegant, each sentence

came to me briefly worded, but most expressive; full
of excellent counsel to the boy, tenderly bequeath-
ing "mother and Lizzie" to his care, and bidding him
good bye in words the sadder for their simplicity. He
added a few lines, with steady hand, and, as I sealed it,
said, with a patient sort of sigh, "I hope the answer
will come in time for me to see it;" then, turning
away his face, laid the flowers against his lips, as if to
hide some quiver of emotion at the thought of such
a sudden sundering of all the dear home ties.

These things had happened two days before; now
John was dying, and the letter had not come. I had
been summoned to many deathbeds in my life, but to
none that made my heart ache as it did then, since
my mother called me to watch the departure of a spirit
akin to this in its gentleness and patient strength.
As I went in, John stretched out both hands:

"I know you'd come! I guess I'm moving on,
ma'am."

He was; and so rapidly that, even while he spoke,
over his face I saw the gray veil falling that no
human hand can lift. I sat down by him, wiped the
drops from his forehead, stirred the air about him
with the slow wave of a fan, and waited to help him
die. He stood in sore need of help—and I could do
so little; for, as the doctor had foretold, the strong
body rebelled against death, and fought every inch
of the way, forcing him to draw each breath with a
spasm, and clench his hands with an imploring

look, as if he asked, "How long must I endure this, and be still!" For hours he suffered dumbly, without a moment's respite, or a moment's murmuring; his limbs grew cold, his face damp, his lips white, and, again and again, he tore the covering off his breast, as if the lightest weight added to his agony; yet through it all, his eyes never lost their perfect serenity, and the man's soul seemed to sit therein, undaunted by the ills that vexed his flesh.

One by one, the men woke, and round the room appeared a circle of pale faces and watchful eyes, full of awe and pity; for, though a stranger, John was beloved by all. Each man there had wondered at his patience, respected his piety, admired his fortitude, and now lamented his hard death; for the influence of an upright nature had made itself deeply felt, even in one little week. Presently, the Jonathan who so loved this comely David, came creeping from his bed for a last look and word. The kind soul was full of trouble, as the choke in his voice, the grasp of his hand, betrayed; but there were no tears, and the farewell of the friends was the more touching for its brevity.

"Old boy, how are you?" faltered the one.

"Most through, thank heaven!" whispered the other.

"Can I say or do anything for you anywheres?"

"Take my things home, and tell them that I did my best."

"I will! I will!"

"Good bye, Ned."

"Good bye, John, good bye!"

They kissed each other, tenderly as women, and so parted, for poor Ned could not stay to see his comrade die. For a little while, there was no sound in the room but the drip of water, from a stump or two, and John's distressful gasps, as he slowly breathed his life away. I thought him nearly gone, and had just laid down the fan, believing its help to be no longer needed, when suddenly he rose up in his bed, and cried out with a bitter cry that broke the silence, sharply startling every one with its agonized appeal:

"For God's sake, give me air!"

It was the only cry pain or death had wrung from him, the only boon he had asked; and none of us could grant it, for all the airs that blew were useless now. Dan flung up the window. The first red streak of dawn was warming the gray east, a herald of the coming sun; John saw it, and with the love of light which lingers in us to the end, seemed to read in it a sign of hope of help, for, over his whole face there broke that mysterious expression, brighter than any smile, which often comes to eyes that look their last. He laid himself gently down; and, stretching out his strong right arm, as if to grasp and bring the blessed air to his lips in a fuller flow, lapsed into a merciful unconsciousness, which assured us that for him suffering was forever past. He died then; for, though the heavy breaths still tore their way up for a little longer, they were but the waves of an ebbing tide that beat unfelt against the wreck, which an immortal voyager had deserted with a smile. He never spoke again, but to the end held my hand close, so close that when he was asleep at last, I could not draw it away. Dan helped me, warning me as he did so that it was unsafe for dead and living flesh to lie so long together; but though my hand was strangely cold and stiff, and four white marks remained across its back, even when warmth and color had returned elsewhere, I could not but be glad that, through its touch, the presence of human sympathy, perhaps, had lightened that hard hour.

When they had made him ready for the grave, John lay in state for half an hour, a thing which seldom happened in that busy place; but a universal sentiment of reverence and affection seemed to fill the hearts of all who had known or heard of him; and when the rumor of his death went through the house, always astir, many came to see him, and I felt a tender sort of pride in my lost patient; for he looked a most heroic figure, lying there stately and still as the statue of some young knight asleep upon his tomb. The lovely expression which so often beautifies dead faces, soon replaced the marks of pain, and I longed for those who loved him best to see him when half an hour's acquaintance with Death had made them friends. As we stood looking at him, the ward master handed me a letter, saying it had been forgotten the night before. It was John's letter, come just an hour too late to gladden the eyes that had longed and looked for it so eagerly! Yet he had it; for, after I had cut some brown locks for his mother, and taken off the ring to send her, telling how well the talisman had done its work, I kissed this good son for her sake, and laid the letter in his hand, still folded as when I drew my own away, feeling that its place was there, and making myself happy with the thought, that, even in his solitary place in the "Government Lot," he would not be without some token of the love which makes life beautiful and outlives death. Then I left him, glad to have known so genuine a man, and carrying with me an enduring memory of the brave Virginia blacksmith, as he lay serenely waiting for the dawn of that long day which knows no night.

Vicksburg During the Trouble

[**MARK TWAIN**]

We used to plow past the lofty hill-city, Vicksburg, down-stream; but we cannot do that now. A cut-off has made a country town of it, like Osceola, St. Genevieve, and several others. There is currentless water—also a big island—in front of Vicksburg now. You come down the river the other side of the island, then turn and come up to the town; that is, in high water: in low water you can't come up, but must land some distance below it.

Signs and scars still remain, as reminders of Vicksburg's tremendous war experiences; earthworks, trees crippled by the cannon balls, cave-refuges in the clay precipices, etc. The caves did good service during the six weeks' bombardment of the city—May 8 to July 4, 1863. They were used by the non-combatants—mainly by the women and children; not to live in constantly, but to fly to for safety on occasion. They were mere holes, tunnels, driven into the perpendicular clay bank, then branched Y shape, within the hill. Life in Vicksburg, during the six weeks was perhaps—but wait; here are some materials out of which to reproduce it:—

Population, twenty-seven thousand soldiers and three thousand non-combatants; the city utterly cut off from the world—walled solidly in, the frontage by gunboats, the rear by soldiers and batteries; hence, no buying and selling with the outside; no passing to and fro; no God-speeding a parting guest, no welcoming a coming one; no printed acres of world-wide news to be read at breakfast, mornings—a tedious dull absence of such matter, instead; hence, also, no running to see steamboats smoking into view in the distance up or down, and plowing toward the town—for none came, the river lay vacant and undisturbed; no rush and turmoil around the railway station, no struggling over bewildered swarms of passengers by noisy mobs of hackmen—all quiet there; flour two hundred dollars a barrel, sugar thirty, corn ten dollars a bushel, bacon five dollars a pound, rum a hundred dollars a gallon; other things in proportion: consequently, no roar and racket of drays and carriages tearing along the streets; nothing for them to do, among that handful of non-combatants of exhausted means; at three o'clock in the morning, silence; silence so dead that

the measured tramp of a sentinel can be heard a seemingly impossible distance; out of hearing of this lonely
sound, perhaps the stillness is absolute: all in a moment
come ground-shaking thunder-crashes of artillery,
the sky is cobwebbed with the crisscrossing red
lines streaming from soaring bomb-shells, and a rain
of iron fragments descends upon the city; descends
upon the empty streets: streets which are not empty
a moment later, but mottled with dim figures of frantic women and children scurrying from home and
bed toward the cave dungeons—encouraged by the
humorous grim soldiery, who shout "Rats, to your
holes!" and laugh.

The cannon-thunder rages, shells scream and crash
overhead, the iron rain pours down, one hour, two
hours, three, possibly six, then stops; silence follows,
but the streets are still empty; the silence continues;
by-and-bye a head projects from a cave here and there
and yonder, and reconnoitres, cautiously; the silence
still continuing, bodies follow heads, and jaded, half
smothered creatures group themselves about, stretch
their cramped limbs, draw in deep draughts of the
grateful fresh air, gossip with the neighbors from
the next cave; maybe straggle off home presently,
or take a lounge through the town, if the stillness continues; and will scurry to the holes again, by-and-bye,
when the war-tempest breaks forth once more.

There being but three thousand of these cave-
dwellers—merely the population of a village—would

they not come to know each other, after a week or two, and familiarly; insomuch that the fortunate or unfortunate experiences of one would be of interest to all?

Those are the materials furnished by history. From them might not almost anybody reproduce for himself the life of that time in Vicksburg? Could you, who did not experience it, come nearer to reproducing it to the imagination of another non-participant than could a Vicksburger who did experience it? It seems impossible; and yet there are reasons why it might not really be. When one makes his first voyage in a ship, it is an experience which multitudinously bristles with striking novelties; novelties which are in such sharp contrast with all this person's former experiences that they take a seemingly deathless grip upon his imagination and memory. By tongue or pen he can make a landsman live that strange and stirring voyage over with him; make him see it all and feel it all. But if he wait? If he make ten voyages in succession—what then? Why, the thing has lost color, snap, surprise; and has become commonplace. The man would have nothing to tell that would quicken a landsman's pulse.

Years ago, I talked with a couple of the Vicksburg non-combatants—a man and his wife. Left to tell their story in their own way, those people told it without fire, almost without interest.

A week of their wonderful life there would have made their tongues eloquent forever perhaps; but they had six weeks of it, and that wore the novelty all out; they got used to being bomb-shelled out of home and into the ground; the matter became commonplace. After that, the possibility of their ever being startlingly interesting in their talks about it was gone. What the man said was to this effect:—

"It got to be Sunday all the time. Seven Sundays in the week—to us, anyway. We hadn't anything to do, and time hung heavy. Seven Sundays, and all of them broken up at one time or another, in the day or in the night, by a few hours of the awful storm of fire and thunder and iron. At first we used to shin for the holes a good deal faster than we did afterwards. The first time, I forgot the children, and Maria fetched them both along. When she was all safe in the cave she fainted. Two or three weeks afterwards, when she was running for the holes, one morning, through a shell-shower, a big shell burst near her, and covered her all over with dirt, and a piece of the iron carried away her game-bag of false hair from the back of her head. Well, she stopped to get that game-bag before she shoved along again! Was getting used to things already, you see. We all got so that we could tell a good deal about shells; and after that we didn't always go under shelter if it was a light shower. Us men would loaf around and talk; and a man would say, 'There she goes!' and name the kind of shell it was from the sound of it, and go on talking—if there wasn't any danger from it. If a shell was bursting close over us, we stopped talking and stood still;—uncomfortable, yes, but it wasn't safe to move. When it let go, we went on talking again, if nobody hurt—maybe saying, 'That was a ripper!' or some such commonplace comment before we resumed; or, maybe, we would see a shell poising itself away high in the air overhead. In that case, every fellow just whipped out a sudden, 'See you again, gents!' and shoved. Often and often I saw gangs of ladies promenading the streets, looking as cheerful as you please, and keeping an eye canted up watching the shells; and I've seen them stop still when they were uncertain about what a shell was going to do, and wait and make certain; and after that they sa'ntered along again, or lit out for shelter, according to the verdict. Streets in some towns have a litter of pieces of paper, and odds and ends of one sort or another lying around. Ours hadn't; they had *iron* litter. Sometimes a man would gather up all the iron fragments and unbursted shells in his neighborhood, and pile them into a kind of monument in his front yard—a ton of it, sometimes. No glass left; glass couldn't stand such a bombardment; it was all shivered out. Windows of the houses vacant—looked like eyeholes in a skull. *Whole* panes were as scarce as news.

"We had church Sundays. Not many there, along at first; but by-and-bye pretty good turnouts. I've

seen service stop a minute, and everybody sit quiet—
no voice heard, pretty funeral-like then—and all the
more so on account of the awful boom and crash
going on outside and overhead; and pretty soon, when
a body could be heard, service would go on again.
Organs and church-music mixed up with a bombardment is a powerful queer combination—along at first.
Coming out of church, one morning, we had an accident—the only one that happened around me on a
Sunday. I was just having a hearty handshake with a
friend I hadn't seen for a while, and saying, 'Drop
into our cave to-night, after bombardment; we've got
hold of a pint of prime wh—.' Whiskey, I was going
to say, you know, but a shell interrupted. A chunk
of it cut the man's arm off, and left it dangling in
my hand. And do you know the thing that is going to
stick the longest in my memory, and outlast everything else, little and big, I reckon, is the mean thought
I had then? It was 'the whiskey *is saved.*' And yet, don't
you know, it was kind of excusable; because it was as
scarce as diamonds, and we had only just that little;
never had another taste during the siege.

"Sometimes the caves were desperately crowded,
and always hot and close. Sometimes a cave had twenty
or twenty-five people packed into it; no turning-
room for anybody; air so foul, sometimes, you couldn't
have made a candle burn in it. A child was born in
one of those caves one night, Think of that; why, it
was like having it born in a trunk.

"Twice we had sixteen people in our cave; and a number of times we had a dozen. Pretty suffocating in there. We always had eight; eight belonged there. Hunger and misery and sickness and fright and sorrow, and I don't know what all, got so loaded into them that none of them were ever rightly their old selves after the siege. They all died but three of us within a couple of years. One night a shell burst in front of the hole and caved it in and stopped it up. It was lively times, for a while, digging out. Some of us came near smothering. After that we made two openings—ought to have thought of it at first.

"Mule meat. No, we only got down to that the last day or two. Of course it was good; anything is good when you are starving."

This man had kept a diary during—six weeks? No, only the first six days. The first day, eight close pages; the second, five; the third, one—loosely written; the fourth, three or four lines; a line or two the fifth and sixth days; seventh day, diary abandoned; life in terrific Vicksburg having now become commonplace and matter of course.

The war history of Vicksburg has more about it to interest the general reader than that of any other of the river-towns. It is full of variety, full of incident, full of the picturesque. Vicksburg held out longer than any other important river-town, and saw warfare in all its phases, both land and water—the siege, the mine, the assault, the repulse, the bombardment, sickness, captivity, famine.

The most beautiful of all the national cemeteries is here. Over the great gateway is this inscription:—

"Here Rest In Peace 16,600 Who Died For Their Country In The Years 1861 To 1865"

My Cave Life in Vicksburg

[MARY ANN WEBSTER
LOUGHBOROUGH]

From gentlemen who called on the evening of the attack in the rear of the town, we learned that it was quite likely, judging from the movements on the river, that the gunboats would make an attack that night. We remained dressed during the night; once or twice we sprang to our feet, startled by the report of a cannon; but after waiting in the darkness of the veranda for some time, the perfect quiet of the city convinced us that our alarm was needless.

Next day, two or three shells were thrown from the battlefield, exploding near the house. This was our first shock, and a severe one. We did not dare to go in the back part of the house all day.

Some of the servants came and got down by us for protection, while others kept on with their work as if feeling a perfect contempt for the shells.

In the evening we were terrified and much excited by the loud rush and scream of mortar shells; we ran to the small cave near the house, and were in it during the night, by this time wearied and almost stupefied by the loss of sleep.

The caves were plainly becoming a necessity, as some persons had been killed on the street by fragments of shells. The room that I had so lately slept in had been struck by a fragment of a shell during the first night, and a large hole made in the ceiling. I shall never forget my extreme fear during the night, and my utter hopelessness of ever seeing the morning light. Terror stricken, we remained crouched in the cave, while shell after shell followed each other in quick succession. I endeavored by constant prayer to prepare myself for the sudden death I was almost certain awaited me. My heart stood still as we would hear the reports from the guns, and the rushing and fearful sound of the shell as it came toward us. As it neared, the noise became more deafening; the air was full of the rushing sound; pains darted through my temples; my ears were full of the confusing noise; and, as it exploded, the report flashed through my head like an electric shock, leaving me in a quiet state of terror the most painful that I can imagine— cowering in a corner, holding my child to my heart—the only feeling of my life being the choking throbs of my heart that rendered me almost breathless. As singly they fell short, or beyond the cave, I was aroused by a feeling of thankfulness that was of short duration. Again and again the terrible fright came over us in that night.

I saw one fall in the road without the mouth of the cave, like a flame of fire, making the earth tremble, and, with a low, singing sound, the fragments sped on in their work of death.

Morning found us more dead than alive, with blanched faces and trembling lips. We were not reassured on hearing, from a man who took refuge in the cave, that a mortar shell in falling would not consider the thickness of earth above us a circumstance.

Some of the ladies, more courageous by daylight, asked him what he was in there for, if that was the case. He was silenced for an hour, when he left. As the day wore on, and we were still preserved, though the shells came as ever, we were somewhat encouraged.

The next morning we heard that Vicksburg would not in all probability hold out more than a week or two, as the garrison was poorly provisioned; and one of General Pemberton's staff officers told us that the effective force of the garrison, upon being estimated, was found to be fifteen thousand men; General Loring having been cut off after the battle of Black River, with probably ten thousand.

The ladies all cried, "Oh, never surrender!" but after the experience of the night, I really could not tell what I wanted, or what my opinions were.

How often I thought of M—— upon the battle field, and his anxiety for us in the midst of this unanticipated danger, wherein the safety lay entirely on the side of the belligerent gentlemen, who were shelling us so furiously, at least two miles from the city, in the bend of the river near the canal.

So constantly dropped the shells around the city, that the inhabitants all made preparations to live under the ground during the siege. M—— sent over and had a cave made in a hill near by. We seized the opportunity one evening, when the gunners were probably at their supper, for we had a few moments of quiet, to go over and take possession. We were under the care of a friend of M——, who was pay-master on the staff of the same General with whom M—— was Adjutant. We had neighbors on both sides of us; and it would have been an amusing sight to a spectator to witness the domestic scenes presented without by the number of servants preparing the meals under the high bank containing the caves.

Our dining, breakfasting, and supper hours were quite irregular. When the shells were falling fast, the servants came in for safety, and our meals waited for completion some little time; again they would fall slowly, with the lapse of many minutes between, and out would start the cooks to their work.

Some families had light bread made in large quantities, and subsisted on it with milk (provided their cows were not killed from one milking time to another), without any more cooking, until called on to replenish. Though most of us lived on corn bread and bacon, served three times a day, the only luxury of the meal consisting in its warmth, I had some flour, and frequently had some hard, tough biscuit made from it, there being no soda or yeast to be procured. At this time we could, also, procure beef. A gentleman friend was kind enough to offer me his camp bed, a narrow spring mattress, which fitted within the contracted cave very comfortably; another had his tent fly stretched over the mouth of our residence to shield us from the sun; and thus I was the recipient of many favors, and under obligations to many gentlemen of the army for delicate and kind attentions; and, in looking back to my trials at that time, I shall ever remember with gratitude the kindness with which they strove to ward off every deprivation. And so I went regularly to work, keeping house underground. Our new habitation was an excavation made in the earth, and branching six feet from the entrance, forming a cave in the shape of a T. In one of the wings my bed fitted; the other I used as a kind of a dressing room; in this the earth had been cut down a foot or two below the floor of the main cave; I could stand erect here; and when tired of sitting in other portions of my residence, I bowed myself into it, and stood impassively resting at full height one of the variations in the still shell-expectant life. M——'s servant cooked for us under protection of the hill. Our quarters were close, indeed; yet I was more comfortable than I expected I could have been made under the earth in that fashion.

We were safe at least from fragments of shell and they were flying in all directions; though no one seemed to think our cave any protection, should a mortar shell happen to fall directly on top of the ground above us. We had our roof arched and braced, the supports of the bracing taking up much room in our confined quarters. The earth was about five feet thick above, and seemed hard and compact; yet, poor M——, every time he came in, examined it, fearing, amid some of the shocks it sustained, that it might crack and fall upon us.

The Fourteenth at Gettysburg

[HARPER'S WEEKLY]

Come, Fred, tell me all about that glorious fight which, you know, it was just my ill-luck to miss. If it had been such another shipping as we had at Fredericksburg, the Fates would probably have let me be there. I have heard several accounts, and know the regiment did nobly; but the boys all get so excited telling about it that I have not yet a clear idea of the fight."

"Here goes, then," said the Adjutant, lighting a fresh cigar. "It will serve to pass away time, which hangs so heavy on our hands in this dreary hospital."

"We were not engaged on the first day of the fight, July 1, 1863, but were on the march for Gettysburg that day. All the afternoon we heard the cannonading growing more and more distinct as we approached the town, and as we came on the field at night learned that the First and Eleventh corps had fought hard, suffered much, and been driven back outside the town with the loss of Major-General Reynolds, who, it was generally said, brought on an engagement too hastily with Lee's whole army. We bivouacked on the field that night.

"About nine o'clock the next morning we moved up to the front, and by ten o'clock the enemy's shells were falling around us. Captain Coit had a narrow escape here. We had just stacked arms and were resting, when a runaway horse, frightened by the shelling, came full tilt at him; 'twas 'heavy cavalry' against 'light infantry;' but Coit had presence of mind enough to draw his sword and bringing it to a point it entered the animal's belly. The shock knocked Coit over, and he was picked up senseless with a terribly battered face, and carried to the rear."

"By-the-way, Fred, is it not singular that he should have recovered so quickly and completely from such a severe blow?"

"Indeed it is. He is as handsome as ever; but to go on. At four o'clock in the afternoon we moved up to support a battery, and here we lay all night. About dark Captain Broatch went out with the pickets. Though under artillery fire all day we were not really engaged, as we did not fire a gun. Some of our pickets, unfortunately going too far to the front, were taken prisoners during the night.

"At about five o'clock on the morning of the 3d Captain Townsend went out with companies B and D and relieved Broatch. As soon as he got out Townsend advanced his men as skirmishers some three hundred yards beyond the regiment, which moved up to the impromptu rifle-pits, which were formed partially by a stone-wall and partially by a rail fence. Just as soon as our skirmishers were posted they began firing at the rebel skirmishers, and kept it up all day, until the grand attack in the afternoon. Before they had been out twenty minutes, Corporal Huxham, of Company B, was instantly killed by a rebel bullet. It was not discovered until another of our skirmishers, getting out of ammunition, went up to him, saying, 'Sam, let me have some cartridges?' Receiving no answer, he stooped down and discovered that a bullet had entered the poor fellow's mouth and gone out at the back of his head, killing the brave, Chancellorsville-scarred, corporal so quickly that he never knew what hurt him. Presently Captain Moore was ordered down with four companies into a lot near by, to drive the rebel sharpshooters out of a house and barn from whence they were constantly picking off our men. Moore went down on a double-quick, and, as usual, ahead of his men; he was first man in the barn, and as he entered the Butternuts were already jumping out. Moore and his men soon cleared the barn and then started for the house. Here that big sergeant in Company J (Norton) sprang in at the front door just in time to catch a bullet in his thigh, from a reb watching at the back;

but that reb did not live long to brag of it, one of our boys taking him 'on the wing.' Moore soon cleared the house out and went back with his men. Later in the day rebs again occupied the house, and Major Ellis took the regiment and drove them out, burning the house, so as not to be bothered by any more concealed sharp-shooters in it."

"Yes, I know the Major don't like to do a thing but once, so he always does it thoroughly the first."

"It was in these charges for the possession of that house we lost more officers and men than in all the rest of the fight.

"About one o'clock in the afternoon the enemy, who had been silent so long that the boys were cooking coffee, smoking, sleeping, etc., suddenly opened all their batteries of reserve artillery upon the position held by our corps (the Second). First one great gun spoke, then, as if it had been the signal for the commencement of an artillery conversation, the whole hundred and twenty or more opened their mouths at once and poured out their thunder. A perfect storm of shot and shell rained around and among us. The boys quickly jumped to their rifles and lay down behind the wall and rail barricade. For two hours this storm of shot and shell continued, and seemed to increase in fury. Good God! I never hear any thing like it, and our regiment has been under fire 'somewhat,' as you know. The ground trembled like an aspen leaf; the air was full of small fragments of lead and iron from the shells. Then the sounds: there was the peculiar *'whoo?—whoo?—whoo-oo?'* of the round shot; the *'which-one?—'which-one?'* of that fiendish Whitworth projectile, and the demoniac shriek of shells. It seemed as if all the devils in hell were holding high carnival. But, strange as it may seem, it was like many other 'sensation doings,' 'great cry and little wool,' as our regiment, and, in fact, the whole corps lost very few men by it, the missiles passing over beyond our position, save the Whitworth projectiles which did not quite reach us, as their single gun of that description was two miles off. Had the enemy had better artillerists at their guns, or a better view of our position, I can not say what would have been the final result; but certain it is, nothing mortal could have stood that fire long, had it been better directed, and if our corps had broken that day, Gettysburg would have been a lost battle, and General Lee, instead of Heintzelman, the commanding officer in this District of Columbia today.

"About three p.m. the enemy's fire slackened, died away, and the smoke lifted to disclose a corps of the rebel 'Grand Army of Northern Virginia,' advancing across the long level plain in our front, in three magnificent lines of battle, with the troops massed in close column by division on both flanks. How splendidly they looked! Our skirmishers, who had staid at their posts through all, gave them volley after volley as they came on, until Captain Townsend was ordered to bring his men in, which he did in admirable order; his men, loading and firing all the way, came in steadily and coolly—all that were left of them, for a good half of them were killed or wounded before they reached the regiment.

"On, on came the rebels, with colors flying and bayonets gleaming in the sunlight, keeping their lines as straight as if on parade: over fences and ditches they come, but still their lines never break, and still they come. For a moment all is hush along our lines, as we gaze in silent admiration at these brave rebs; then our division commander, 'Aleck Hayes,' rides up, and, pointing to the last fence the enemy must cross before reaching us, says, 'Don't fire till they get to that fence; then let 'em have.'

"On, on, come the rebs, till we can see the whites of their eyes, and hear their officers command, 'Steady, boys, steady!' They reach the fence, some hundred yards in front of us, when suddenly the command 'Fire!' rings down our line; and, rising as one man, the rifles of the old Second Army Corps ring a death-knell for many a brave heart, in butter-nut dress, worthy of a better cause—a knell that will ring in the hearts of many mothers, sister, and wives, on many a plantation in the once fair and sunny South, where there will be weeping and wailing for the soldier who never returns, who sleeps at Gettysburg. 'Load and fire at will!' Oh Heaven! How we poured our fire into them then—a merciless hail of lead! Their first line wavers, breaks, and runs; some of their color sergeants halt and plant their standards firmly in the ground: they are too well disciplined to leave their colors yet. But they stop only for a moment; then fall back, colors and all. They fall back, but rally, and dress on the other lines, under a tremendous fire from our advancing rifles: rally, and come on again to meet their death. Line after line of rebels come up, deliver their fire, one volley, and they are mown down like the grass of the field. They fall back, form, and come up again, with their battle-flags still waving; but again they are driven back.

"On our right is a break in the line, where a battery has been in position, but, falling short of ammunition, and unable to move it off under such a heavy fire, the gunners have abandoned it to its fate. Some of the rebels gain a footing here. One daring fellow leaps upon the gun, and waves his rebel flag. In an instant a right oblique fire from 'ours,' and a left oblique from the regiment on the left of the position, rolls the ragged rebel and rebel rag in the dust, rolls the determined force back from the gun, and it is ours.

"By-and-by the enemy's lines come up smaller and thinner, break quicker, and are longer in forming. Our boys are wild with excitement, and grow reckless. Lieutenant John Tibbetts stands up yelling like mad, 'Give it to 'em! Give it to 'em!' A bullet enters his arm—that same arm in which he caught two bullets at Antietam; Johnny's game arm drops by his side; he turns quickly to his First Lieutenant, saying, 'I have got another bullet in the same old arm, but I don't care a d—n!' Heaven forgive Johnny! Rebel lead will sometimes bring rebel words with it. All of 'Ours' are carried away with excitement; the Sergeant-Major leaps a wall, dashes down among the rebs, and brings back a battle-flag; others follow our Sergeant-Major; and before the enemy's repulse becomes a rout we of the Fourteenth have six of their battle-flags.

"Prisoners are brought in by hundreds, officers and men. We pay no attention to them, being too busy sending our leaden messengers after the now flying hosts. One of our prisoners, a rebel officer, turns to me, saying, 'Where are the men we've been fighting?' 'Here,' I answer, pointing down our short thin line. 'Good God!' says he, 'Is that all? I wish I could get back.'"

"Yes," I interrupted, "Townsend told me that when he fell back with his skirmishers and saw the whole length of our one small, thin, little line pitted against those then full lines of the rebels, his heart almost sank within him; but Meade had planned that battle well, and every one of our soldiers told."

"Yes," said Fred, "Meade planned the fight well, and Hancock, Hayes, and in fact all of them fought it well. All through the fight General Hancock might be seen galloping up and down the lines of our bully corps, regardless of the leaden hail all about him; and when finally severely wounded in the hip he was carried a little to the rear, where he lay on his stretcher and still gave his orders.

"The fight was now about over; there was only an occasional shot exchanged between the retreating rebel sharp-shooters and our own men, and I looked about me and took an account of stock. We had lost about seventy killed and wounded and taken prisoners, leaving only a hundred men fit for duty. We had killed treble that number, and taken nearly a brigade of prisoners; six stands of colors, and guns, swords, and pistols without number. For the first time we had been through an action without having an officer killed or fatally wounded, though Tibbetts, Seymour, Stoughton, Snagg, Seward, and Dudley were more or less seriously wounded, and Coit disabled.

"Hardly a man in the regiment had over two or three cartridges left. Dead and wounded rebels were piled up in heaps in front of us, especially in front of Companies A and B, where Sharpe's rifles had done effective work.

"It was a great victory. 'Fredericksburg on the other leg,' as the boys said.

The rebel prisoners told us their leaders assured them that they would only meet the Pennsylvania militia; but when they saw that d——d ace of clubs (the trefoil badge of the Second Corps), a cry went through their lines—'the Army of the Potomac, by Heaven!'

"So ended the battle of Gettysburg, and the sun sank to rest that night on a battle-field that had proved that the Army of the Potomac could and would save the people of the North from invasion whenever and wherever they may be assailed.

> *"'Long shall the tale be told,*
> *Yea, when our babes are old.'"*

"Pshaw, Fred! you are getting sentimental. Let's go out in the air and have another cigar."

Completing My Disguise

[S. EMMA E. EDMONDS]

After hastily partaking of a slight repast, which I could scarcely term breakfast, I commenced immediate preparations to leave the house. Upon examining the basket in which I found the tea on my arrival, I found a number of articles which assisted me much in assuming a more perfect disguise. There was mustard, pepper, an old pair of green spectacles, and a bottle of red ink. Of the mustard I made a strong plaster about the size of a dollar, and tied it on one side of my face until it blistered thoroughly; with the ink I painted a red line around my eyes, and after giving my pale complexion a deep tinge with some ochre which I found in a closet, I put on my green glasses and my Irish hood, which came over my face about six inches.

I then made the tour of the house from garret to cellar, to find all the household fixings which an

Irishwoman would be supposed to carry with her in such an emergency—for I expected to be searched before I was admitted through the lines. I packed both my baskets, for I had two now, and was ready for another start. But before leaving I thought best to bury my pistol and every article in my possession which could in any way induce suspicion. Then taking a farewell look at the beautiful features of the dead, I left the house, going directly the nearest road to the rebel picket line. I felt perfectly safe in doing so, for the rebel soldier's watch was a sufficient passport in daylight, and a message for Major McKee would insure me civility at least.

I followed the Richmond road about five miles before meeting or seeing any one. At length I saw a sentinel in the distance, but before he observed me I sat down to rest and prepare my mind for the coming interview. While thus waiting to have my courage reinforced, I took from my basket the black pepper and sprinkled a little of it on my pocket handkerchief, which I applied to my eyes. The effect was all I could have desired, for taking a view of my prepossessing countenance in the small mirror which I always carried with me, I perceived that my eyes had a fine tender expression, which added very much to the beauty of their red borders. I was reminded of poor Leah of old who failed to secure the affection of her husband in consequence of a similar blemish, and thought myself safe from the slightest approach to admiration on the part of the chivalry.

I now resumed my journey, and displayed a flag of truce, a piece of a cotton window curtain which I brought from the house at which I had stopped over night. As I came nearer the picket-guard signaled me to advance, which I did as fast as I could under circumstances, being encumbered with two heavy baskets packed full of earthenware, clothing, quilts, etc. Upon coming up to the guard, instead of being dismayed at his formidable appearance, I felt rejoiced, for there stood before me an immense specimen of a jolly Englishman, with a bland smile on his good-natured face, provoked, I presume, by the supremely ludicrous figure I presented.

He mildly questioned me with regard to my hopes and fears, whence I came and whither I was going, and if I had seen any Yankees. My sorrowful story was soon told. My peppery handkerchief was freely applied to my eyes, and the tears ran down my face without the least effort on my part. The good-natured guard's sympathy was excited, more especially as I was a foreigner like himself, and he told me I could pass along and go just wherever I pleased, so far as he was concerned, adding in a sad tone, "I wish I was hat 'ome with my family, hand then Jeff. Davis hand the Confederacy might go to 'ell for hall me. Hinglishmen 'ave no business 'ere." I mentally exclaimed, "Good for you—you are one after my own heart," but I replied to the English-man's patriotic speech after the following manner: "Och, indade I wish yez was all at home wid yer families, barrin' them as have no families; an sure its we poor craythurs of wimen that's heartbroken intirely, an fairly kilt wid this onnathral war;" and here my eyes were again carefully wiped with my handkerchief.

After thanking the picket-guard for his kindness, I went on my way toward the rebel camp. I had not gone far when the guard called me back and advised me not to stay in camp overnight, for, said he, "One of our spies has just come in and reported that the Yankees have finished the bridges across the Chick-ahominy, and intend to attack us either to-day or to-night, but Jackson and Lee are ready for them." He went on to tell me how many masked batteries they had prepared, and said he, "There is one," pointing to a brush heap by the roadside, "that will give them fits if they come this way."

Feeling somewhat in a hurry, I started once more for camp. I concluded after getting through the lines that I could dispense with one of my bas-kets, so setting one of them down under a tree I felt much more comfortable, and was not quite so conspicuous an object going into camp. I went directly to headquarters and inquired for Major McKee. I was told that he would not be there before evening, and my informant drawled out after me, "He's gone to set a trap for the d—d Yankees."

I made up my mind at once that I must find out as much as possible before night, and make my way back before the impending battle came on. Upon looking around the camp I saw a shanty where some negro women were cooking meat. I went and told them that I was hungry and would like to have something to eat. "Oh yes, honey, we'se got lots o' meat and bread, but haint got no salt; but reckon ye can eat it without." So saying an old auntie brought me a piece of boiled fresh beef and some bread; but I could not make out what the bread was made of; as near as I could guess, however, it was made of boiled rice and corn-meal, and that also was without salt.

I thought it would be well to look a little smarter before I presented myself at headquarters again, lest I might not meet with that confidence which I felt it was important for me to secure. My patched and painted face made it impossible for any one to define the expression of my countenance. My blistered cheek was becoming very painful in consequence of the drawing of the court plaster. I took off my glasses and bathed my face in clear, cold water, which did not remove much of the color, but made me a shade more like myself; then I succeeded in getting one of the women to go to the doctor's quarters and get me some unguent, or simple cerate, with which I dressed the blister. My eyes were sufficiently disfigured by this time to dispense with the glasses, so putting them in my basket I laid them aside for another occasion. There was no difficulty in finding out the force of the enemy or their plans for the coming battle, for every one, men and women, seemed to think and talk of nothing else.

Five o'clock came, and with it Major McKee. I lost no time in presenting myself before his majorship, and with a profound Irish courtesy I made known my business, and delivered the watch and package. I did not require any black pepper now to assist the lachrymal glands in performing their duty, for the sad mementoes which I had just delivered to the major so forcibly reminded me of the scenes of the past night that I could not refrain from weeping. The major, rough and stern as he was, sat there with his face between his hands and sobbed like a child. Soon he rose to his feet, surveyed me from head to foot, and said, "You are a faithful woman, and you shall be rewarded."

He then asked: "Can you go direct to that house, and show my men where Allen's body is?" I answered in the affirmative—whereupon he handed me a ten dollar Federal bill, saying, as he did so: "If you succeed in finding the house, I will give you as much more." I thanked him, but positively declined taking the money. He did not seem to understand the philosophy of a person in my circumstances refusing money, and when I looked at him again his face

wore a doubtful, puzzled expression, which alarmed
me. I was actually frightened, and bursting into a passionate fit of weeping, I exclaimed vehemently: "Oh,
Gineral, forgive me! but me conshins wud niver
give me pace in this world nor in the nixt, if I wud
take money for carying the dyin missage for that
swate boy that's dead and gone—God rest his soul.
Och, indade, indade I nivir cud do sich a mane thing,
if I im a poor woman." The major sccmcd satisfied,
and told me to wait until he returned with a detachment of men.

When he returned with the men, I told him that I
did not feel able to walk that distance, and requested
him to let me have a horse, stating the fact that I had
been sick for several days, and had slept but little the
night before. He did not answer a word, but ordered
a horse saddled immediately, which was led forward
by a colored boy, who assisted me to mount. I really
felt mean, and for the first time since I had acted in
the capacity of spy, I despised myself for the very
act which I was about to perform. I must betray the
confidence which that man reposed in me. He was
too generous to harbor a suspicion against me, and
thus furnished me the very means of betraying him.

This feeling did not last long, however, for as we
started on our mission he said to his men: "Now,
boys, bring back the body of Captain Hall, if you
have to walk through Yankee blood to the knees."
That speech eased my conscience considerably. I was

surprised to hear him say "Captain Hall," for I did not know until then that he was an officer. There was nothing about his uniform or person to indicate his rank, and I had supposed he was a private soldier.

We made our way toward the house very cautiously, lest we should be surprised by the Federals. I rode at the head of the little band of rebels as guide, not knowing but that I was leading them into the jaws of death every step we advanced, and if so it would probably be death for me as well as for them. Thus we traveled those five miles, silently, thoughtfully, and stealthily. The sun had gone down behind the western hills, and the deepening shadows were fast gathering around us as we came in sight of the little white cottage in the forest, where I had so recently spent such a strangely, awfully solemn night.

The little detachment halted to rest, and to make arrangements before approaching the house. This detachment consisted of twenty-four men, under a sergeant and a corporal. The men were divided into squads, each of which was to take its turn at carrying the body of their late Captain upon a stretcher, which they had brought for that purpose. As we drew near, and saw no sign of an approaching enemy, they regretted that they had not brought an ambulance; but I did not regret it, for the present arrangement suited me exactly. Having settled things satisfactorily among themselves, we again resumed our march and were soon at the gate. The sergeant then ordered the corporal to proceed to the house with a squad of men and bring out the corpse, while he stationed the remaining men to guard all the approaches to the house.

He then asked me to ride down the road a little way, and if I should see or hear anything of the Yankees to ride back as fast as possible and let them know. I assented, and joyfully complied with the first part of his request. This was a very pleasant duty assigned me, for which I mentally thanked the sergeant a thousand times. I turned and rode slowly down the road, but not "seeing or hearing anything of the Yankees," I thought it best to keep on in that direction until I did. I was like the Zouave, after the battle of Bull Run, who said he was ordered to retreat, but not being ordered to halt at any particular place, he preferred to keep on until he reached New York. So I preferred to keep on until I reached the Chickahominy, where I reported progress to the Federal general.

I had no desire to have that little escort captured, and consequently said nothing about it in my report; so the sergeant, with his men, were permitted to return to the rebel camp unmolested, bearing with them the remains of their beloved captain. After getting out of sight of the rebel guards, I made that horse go over the ground about as fast, I think, as he ever did before which seemed to give him a bad impression of Yankees in general, and of me in particular, for ever after that night, it was as much as a person's life was worth to saddle him; at every attempt he would kick and bite most savagely.

The next day the following order was issued: "Upon advancing beyond the Chickahominy the troops will go prepared for battle at a moment's notice, and will be entirely unencumbered, with the exception of ambulances. All vehicles will be left on the eastern side of the Chickahominy, and carefully packed.

"The men will leave their knapsacks, packed, with the wagons, and will carry three days rations. The arms will be put in perfect order before the troops march, and a careful inspection made of them, as well as of the cartridge-boxes, which in all cases will contain at least forty rounds; twenty additional rounds will be carried by the men in their pockets. Commanders of batteries will see that their limber and caisson-boxes are filled to their utmost capacity.

"Commanders of Army Corps will devote their personal attention to the fulfillment of these orders, and will personally see that the proper arrangements are made for packing and properly guarding the trains and surplus baggage, taking all the steps necessary to insure their being brought promptly to the front when needed; they will also take steps to prevent the ambulances from interfering with the movements of any troops. Sufficient guards and staff-officers will be detailed to carry out these orders. The ammunition-wagons will be in readiness to march to their respective brigades and batteries at a moment's warning, but will not cross the Chickahominy until they are sent for. All quarter-masters and ordnance officers are to remain with their trains.

"In the approaching battle the general commanding trusts that the troops will preserve the discipline which he has been so anxious to enforce, and which they have so generally observed. He calls upon all the officers and soldiers to obey promptly and intelligently all the orders they may receive; let them bear in mind that the Army of the Potomac has never yet been checked, and let them preserve in battle perfect coolness and confidence, the sure forerunners of success. They must keep well together, throw away no shots, but aim carefully and low, and, above all things, rely upon the bayonet. Commanders of regiments are reminded of the great responsibility that rests upon them; upon their coolness, judgment, and discretion, the destinies of their regiments and success of the day will depend."

The Charge in the Lane

[GEORGE WASHINGTON CABLE]

The instant Ferry wheeled at the flaming captain's side you could see he was unwelcome. I heard him tell what we knew of the foe and the ground; I saw him glance back at the blown condition of the speeding column and then say, "You've got them anyhow, Captain; you'll get every man of them without a scratch, only if you will take your time."

But the Captain answered headily: "No, sir! I've tried that twice already; this time I'll cut them in two and be in their rear at one dash! Bring in your company behind mine, if you choose."

Ferry drew back a few ranks but stayed with the column; Quinn had had the toil of the chase, he should have also the glory of the fight. So Ferry sent Gholson—whose horsemanship won a cheer from the passing Louisianians as he cleared the roadside

fence—across to Quinn, bidding the Lieutenant
slacken speed and count himself a reserve. And
then into the broad lane between grove and woods-
pasture, with the charging yell, the Louisianians
thundered. Ah! but my Creole gentleman was a sight,
with his straight blade lifted in air and his face turned
back on us aglow with the joy of battle! I was huz-
zaing back at him and we were passing the front gate
of the grove avenue, when down through it came
from the house, with a tremor of echoes, the first
shot; a shot and then a woman's scream, and his blazing eyes said to me, "He is there! That was Oliver!"

There was no time for speech. The shot was not a
signal, yet on the instant and in our very teeth, on
our right and our left, the cross-fire of the hidden
and waiting foe flashed and pealed, and left and
right, a life for a life, our carbines answered from
the saddle. For a moment the odds against us were
awful. In an instant the road was so full of fallen
horses and dismounted men that the jaded column
faltered in confusion. Our cunning enemy, seeing us
charge in column, had swung the two extremes of
their line forward and inward. So, crouching and firing upon us mounted, each half could fire toward
the other with impunity, and what bullets missed
their mark buzzed and whined about our ears and
pecked the top rails of either fence like hail on a
window. A wounded horse drove mine back upon
his haunches and caused him to plant a hoof full on

the breast of one of our Louisianians stretched dead on his back as though he had lain there for an hour. Another man, pale, dazed, unhurt, stood on the ground, unaware that he was under point-blank fire, holding by the bits his beautiful horse, that pawed the earth majestically and at every second or third breath blew from his flapping nostrils a cloud of scarlet spray. They blocked up half the road. As we swerved round them the horse of the company's first lieutenant slid forward and downward with knees and nose in the dust, hurling his rider into a lock of the fence, and the rider rose and rushed to the road again barely in time to catch a glittering form that dropped rein and sword and reeled backward from the saddle. It was his captain, shot through the breast. An instant later our tangled column parted to right and left, dashed into the locks of the two fences, sprang to the ground, and began to repay the enemy in the coin of their own issue. Only a dozen or so did otherwise, and it was my luck to be one of these. Espying Ned Ferry at the very front, in the road, standing in his stirrups and shouting back for followers to carry the charge on through, we spurred toward him and he turned and led. Then what was my next fortune but to see, astride of my stolen horse, the towering leader of the foe, Captain Jewett.

He came into the road a few rods ahead of us through a gap his men had earlier made opposite the big white gate. He answered our fierce halloo, as he crossed, by a pistol-shot at Ferry, but Ferry only glanced around at me and pointed after him with his sword. A number of blue-coats afoot followed him to the gap but at our onset scattered backward, sturdily returning our fire. Into the gap and into the enemy's left rear went Ferry and his horsemen, but I turned the other way and spurred through the woods-pasture gate after the Federal leader, he on my horse and I on his. Down the highway, on either side, stood his brave men's horses in the angles of the worm-fence, and two or three horse-holders took a shot at me as I sped in after the man who was bent on reaching the right of his divided force before Quinn should strike it, as I was bent on foiling him. Twice I fired at his shapely back, and twice, while he kept his speed among the tree-trunks, he looked back at me as coolly as at an odd passer-by and sent me a ball from his revolver. A few more bonds carried him near enough to his force to shout his commands, but half a hundred cheers suddenly resounded in the depth of the woods-pasture, and Quinn and his men charged upon the foe's right and rear. I joined the shout and the shouters; in a moment the enemy were throwing down their arms, and I turned to regain the road to the pond. For I had marked Jewett burst through Quinn's line and with a score of shots ringing after him make one last brave dash—for escape. Others, pursuing him, bent northward, but my instinct was right, his last hope was for his horse-holders, and at a sharp angle of the by-road, where it reached the pond, exactly where Camille and I had stood not an hour before, I came abruptly upon Cricket—riderless. I seized his rein, and as I bent and snapped the halter of one horse on the snaffle of the other I saw the missing horseman. Leaping from the saddle I ran to him. He was lying on his face in the shallow water where General Austin and his staff had so gaily halted a short while before, and as I caught sight of him he rolled upon his back and tried to lift his bemired head. . . .

I dropped to my knee in the reddening pool and passed my arm under his head.

"Thank you," he said, and repeated the word as I wet my handkerchief and wiped the mire from his face; "thank you;—no, no,"—I was opening his shirt—"that's useless; get me where you can turn me over; you've hit me in the back, my lad."

"I?—I hit you? Oh, Captain Jewett, thank God, I didn't hit you at all!"

"What's the difference, boy; you didn't aim to miss, did you? I didn't. It's not my only hurt; I think I broke something inside when I fell from the sad'—ah! that's *your* bugle, isn't it? It's my last fight—oh, the devil! My good boy, don't begin to cry again; war's war; give me some water. . . . Thank you! And now, if you don't want me to bleed to death get me out of this slop, and—yes,— easy!—that's it—easy—oh, God! Oh, let me down, boy, let me down, *you're killing me!* Oh!—" he fainted away.

With his unconscious head still on my arm I faced toward the hundred after-sounds of the fray and hallooed for help. To my surprise it promptly came. Three blundering boys we were who lifted him into the saddle and bore him to the house reeling and moaning astride of Cricket, the poor beast half dead with hard going. The sinking sun was as red as October when we issued into the highroad and moved up it to the grove gate through the bloody wreckage of the fray. . . .

Intensification of Suffering and Hatred

[PHOEBE YATES PEMBER]

Now during the summer of 1864 began what is really meant by "war," for privations had to be endured which tried body and soul, and which temper and patience had to meet unflinchingly day and night. A growing want of confidence was forced upon the mind; and with doubts which though unexpressed were felt as to the ultimate success of our cause, there came into play the antagonistic qualities of human nature.

The money worthless, and a weak Congress and weaker financier failing to make it much more valuable than the paper it was printed on; the former refusing to the last to raise the hospital fund to meet the depreciation. Everything furnished through government contracts of the very poorest description, perhaps necessarily so from the difficulty of finding any supply.

The railroads were cut so constantly that what had been carefully collected in the country in the form of poultry and vegetables by hospital agents would be rendered unfit for use by the time the connection would be restored. The inducements for theft were great in this season of scarcity of food and clothing. The pathetic appeals made for the coarsest meal by starving men all wore upon the health and strength of those exposed to the strain, and made life weary and hopeless.

The rations became so small about this time that every ounce of flour was valuable, and there were days when it was necessary to refuse with aching heart and brimming eyes the request of decent, manly-looking fellows for a piece of dry corn-bread. If given it would have robbed the rightful owner of part of his scanty rations. After the flour or meal had been made into bread, it was almost ludicrous to see with what painful solicitude Miss G. and myself would count the rolls, or hold a council over the pans of corn-bread, measuring with a string how large we could afford to cut the squares, to be apportioned to a certain number.

Sometimes when from the causes above stated, the supplies were not issued as usual, invention had to be taxed to an extreme, and every available article in our pantry brought into requisition. We had constantly to fall back upon dried applies and rice for convalescing appetites, and herb-tea and arrowroot for the very ill. There was only one way of making the last at all palatable, and that was by drenching it with whiskey.

Long abstinence in the field from everything that could be considered, even then, a delicacy, had exaggerated the fancy of sick men for any particular article of food they wanted into a passion; and they begged for such peculiar dishes that surgeons and nurses might well be puzzled. The greatest difficulty in granting these desires was that tastes became contagious, and whatever one patient asked for, his neighbor and the one next to him, and so on throughout the wards, craved also, and it was impossible to decide upon whom to draw a check.

No one unacquainted with our domestic relations can appreciate the difficulties under which we labored. Stoves in any degree of newness or usefulness we did not have; they were rare and expensive luxuries. As may be supposed, they were not the most convenient articles in the world to pack away in blockade-running vessels; and the trouble and expense of land transportation also seriously affected the quality of the wood for fuel furnished us. Timber which had been condemned heretofore as unfit for use, light, soggy and decayed, became the only quality available. The bacon, too, cured the first two years of the war, when salt commanded an enormous price, in most cases was spoilt, from the economy used in preparing that article; and bacon was one of the sinews of war.

We kept up brave hearts, and said we could eat the simplest fare, and wear the coarsest clothing, but there was absolutely nothing to be bought that did not rank as a luxury. It was wasting time and brain to attempt to economize, so we bent to the full force of that wise precept, "Sufficient for the day is the evil thereof."

There really was a great deal of heroism displayed when looking back, at the calm courage with which I learned to count the number of mouths to be fed daily, and then contemplating the food, calculate not how much but how little each man could be satisfied with. War may be glorious in all its panoply and pride, when in the field opposing armies meet and strive for victory; but battles fought by starving the sick and wounded—by crushing in by main force day by day all the necessities of human nature, make victories hardly worth the name.

Another of my local troubles were the rats, who felt the times, and waxed strong and cunning, defying all attempts to entrap them, and skillfully levying blackmail upon us day by day, and night after night. Hunger had educated their minds and sharpened their reasoning faculties. Other vermin, the change of seasons would rid us of, but the coldest day in winter, and the hottest in summer, made no apparent difference in their vivacious strategy.

They examined traps with the air of connoisseurs, sometimes springing them from a safe position, and

kicked over the bread spread with butter and strych-
nine to show their contempt for such underhand
warfare. The men related wonderful rat-stories not
well enough authenticated to put on record, but
their gourmands ate all the poultices applied during
the night to the sick, and dragged away the pads
stuffed with bran from under the arms and legs of
the wounded.

They even performed a surgical operation which
would have entitled any of them to pass the board. A
Virginian had been wounded in the very center of
the instep of his left foot. The hole made was large,
and the wound sloughed fearfully around a great
lump of proud flesh which had formed in the center
like an island. The surgeons feared to remove this
mass, as it might be connected with the nerves of the
foot, and lockjaw might ensue. Poor Patterson would
sit on his bed all day gazing at his lame foot and
bathing it with a rueful face, which had brightened
amazingly one morning when I paid him a visit. He
exhibited it with great glee, the little island gone, and
a deep hollow left, but the wound washed clean and
looking healthy.

Some skillful rat surgeon had done him this good
service while in the search for luxuries, and he only
knew that on awaking in the morning he had found
the operation performed. I never had but one personal interview with any of them. An ancient gray
gentleman, who looked a hundred years old, both

in years and depravity, would eat nothing but butter, when that article was twenty dollars a pound;
so finding all means of getting rid of him fail
through his superior intelligence, I caught him
with a fish-hook, well baited with a lump of his
favorite butter, dropped into his domicile under
the kitchen floor.

Epicures sometimes managed to entrap them and
secure a nice broil for supper, declaring that their
flesh was superior to squirrel meat; but never having
tasted it, I cannot add my testimony to its merits.
They staid with us to the last, nor did I ever observe
any signs of a desire to change their politics.

Perhaps some curious *gourmet* may wish a recipe
for the best mode of cooking them. The rat must be
skinned, cleaned, his head cut off and his body laid
open upon a square board, the legs stretched to
their full extent and secured upon it with small
tacks, then baste with bacon fat and roast before a
good fire quickly like canvas-back ducks.

One of the remarkable features of the war was
the perfect good nature with which the rebels discussed their foes. In no instance up to a certain period
did I hear of any remark that savored of personal
hatred. They fought for a cause and against a power,
and would speak in depreciation of a corps or brigade;
but "they fit us, and we fit them," was the whole
story generally, and till the blowing up of the
mine at Petersburg there was a gay, insouciant style

in their descriptions of the war scenes passing under their observation.

But after that time the sentiment changed from an innate feeling the Southern soldiers had that mining was "a mean trick," as they expressed it. They were not sufficiently versed in military tactics to recognize that stratagem is fair in war . . . The men had heretofore been calm and restrained, particularly before a woman, never using oaths or improper language, but the wounded that were brought in from that fight emulated the talents of Uncle Toby's army in Flanders, and eyes gleamed, and teeth clenched as they showed me the locks of their muskets to which the blood and hair still clung, when after firing, without waiting to re-load, they had clenched the barrels and fought hand to hand. If their accounts could be relied upon, it was a gallant strife and a desperate one, and ghastly wounds bore testimony of the truth of many a tale then told.

Once again the bitter blood showed itself, when, after a skirmish, the foe cut the rail track, so that the wounded could not be brought to the city. Of all the monstrous crimes that war sanctions, this is surely the most sinful. Wounded soldiers without the shelter of a roof, or the comfort of a bed of straw, left exposed to sun, dew, and rain, with hardly the prospect of a warm drink or decent food for days, knowing that comfortable quarters awaited them, all ready prepared, but rendered useless by what seems an unnecessarily cruel act. Was it any wonder that their habitual indifference to suffering gave way, and the soldier cursed loud and deep at a causeless inhumanity, which, if practiced habitually, is worse than savage! When the sufferers at last reached the hospital, their wounds had not been attended to for three days, and the sight of them was shocking.

Busy in my kitchen, seeing that the supply of necessary food was in preparation, I was spared the sight of much of the suffering, but on passing among the ambulances going in and out of the wards I descried seated up on one of them a dilapidated figure, both hands holding his head which was tied up with rags of all descriptions. He appeared to be incapable of talking, but nodded and winked and made motions with head and feet. In the general confusion he had been forgotten, so I took him under my especial charge. He was taken into a ward, seated on a bed, while I stood on a bench to be able to unwind rag after rag from around his head. There was no sensitiveness on his part, for his eye was merry and bright, but when the last came off, what a sight!

Two balls had passed through his cheek and jaw within half an inch of each other, knocking out the teeth on both sides and cutting the tongue in half. The inflammation caused the swelling to be immense, and the absence of all previous attendance, in consequence of the detention of the wounded until the road could be mended, had aggravated the symptoms. There was nothing fatal to be apprehended, but fatal wounds are not always the most trying.

The sight of this was the most sickening my long experience had ever seen. The swollen lips turned out, and the mouth filled with blood, matter, fragments of teeth from amidst all of which the maggots in countless numbers swarmed and writhed, while the smell generated by this putridity was unbearable. Castile soap and soft sponges soon cleansed the offensive cavity, and he was able in an hour to swallow some nourishment he drew through a quill.

The following morning I found him reading the newspaper, and entertaining every one about him by his abortive attempts to make himself understood, and in a week he actually succeeded in doing so. The first request distinctly enunciated was that he wanted a looking-glass to see if his sweetheart would be willing to kiss him when she saw him. We all assured him that she would not be worthy of the name if she would not be delighted to do so.

An order came about this time to clear out the lower wards for the reception of improperly vaccinated patients, who soon after arrived in great numbers. They were dreadfully afflicted objects, many of them with sores so deep and thick upon arms and legs that amputation had to be resorted to, to preserve life. As fast as the eruption would be healed in one spot, it would break out in another, for the blood seemed entirely poisoned. The unfortunate victims bore the infliction as they had borne everything else painful—with calm patience and indifference to suffering. Sometimes a favorable comparison would be made between this and the greater loss of limbs.

No one who was a daily witness to their agonies from this cause, can help feeling indignant at charges made of inhumanity to Federal prisoners of war, who were vaccinated with the same virus; and while on this subject, though it may be outside of the recollections of hospital life, I cannot help stating that on no occasion was the question of rations and medicines to be issued for Federal prisoners discussed in my presence; and circumstances placed me where I had the best opportunity of hearing the truth (living with the wife of a cabinet officer); that good evidence was not given, that the Confederate commissary-general, by order of the government issued to them the same rations it gave its soldiers in the field, and only when reductions of food had to be made in our army, were they also made in the prisons. The question of supplies for them was an open and a vexed one among the people generally, and angry and cruel things were *said;* but every one cognizant of facts in Richmond *knows* that even when General Lee's army lived on corn-meal at times that the prisoners still received their usual rations.

At a cabinet meeting when the Commissary-General Northrop advocated putting the prisoners on the half rations which our soldiers had been obliged to content themselves with for some time, General Lee opposed him on the ground that men animated by companionship and active service could be satisfied with less than prisoners with no hope and leading an inactive life. Mr. Davis sided with him, and the question was settled that night, although in his anger Mr. Northrop accused General Lee of showing this consideration because his son was a prisoner in the enemy's lines.

A Night Ride of the Wounded

[RANDALL PARRISH]

It was a wild, rude scene without, yet in its way typical of a little-understood chapter of Civil War. Moreover it was one with which I was not entirely unacquainted. Years of cavalry scouting, bearing me beyond the patrol lines of the two great armies, had frequently brought me into contact with those various independent, irregular forces which, co-operating with us, often rendered most efficient service by preying on the scattered Federal camps and piercing their lines of communication. Seldom risking an engagement in the open, their policy was rather to dash down upon some outpost or poorly guarded wagon train, and retreat with a rapidity rendering pursuit hopeless. It was partisan warfare, and appealed to many ill-adapted to abide the stricter discipline of regular service. These border rangers would rendezvous under some chosen leader, strike an unexpected blow where weakness had been discovered, then disappear as quickly as they came, oftentimes scattering widely until the call went forth for some fresh assault. It was service not dissimilar to that performed during the Revolutionary struggle by Sumter and Marion in the Carolinas, and added in the aggregate many a day to the contest of the Confederacy.

Among these wild, rough riders between the lines no leader was more favorably known of our army, nor more dreaded by the enemy, than Mosby. Daring to the point of recklessness, yet wary as a fox, counting opposing numbers nothing when weighed against the advantage of surprise, tireless in saddle, audacious in resource, quick to plan and equally quick to execute, he was always where least expected, and it was seldom he failed to win reward for those who rode at his back. Possessing regular rank in the Confederate Army, making report of his operations to the commander-in-chief, his peculiar talent as a partisan leader had won him what was practically an independent command. Knowing him as I did, I was not surprised that he should now have swept suddenly out of the black night upon the very verge of the battle to drive his irritating sting into the hard-earned Federal victory.

An empty army wagon, the "U. S. A." yet conspicuous upon its canvas cover, had been overturned and fired in front of the hospital tent to give light to the raiders. Grouped about beneath the trees, and within the glow of the flames, was a picturesque squad of horsemen, hardy, tough-looking fellows the most of them, their clothing an odd mixture of uniforms, but every man heavily armed and admirably equipped for service. Some remained mounted, lounging carelessly in their saddles, but far the larger number were on foot, their bridle-reins wound about their wrists. All alike appeared alert and ready for any emergency. How many composed the party I was unable to judge with accuracy, as they constantly came and went from out the shadows beyond the circumference of the fire. As all sounds of firing had ceased, I concluded that the work planned had been already accomplished. Undoubtedly, surprised as they were, the small Federal force left to guard this point had been quickly overwhelmed and scattered.

The excitement attendant upon my release had left me for the time being utterly forgetful as to the pain of my wounds, so that weakness alone held me to the blanket upon which I had been left. The night was decidedly chilly, yet I had scarcely begun to feel its discomfort, when a man strode forward from out the nearer group and stood looking down upon me. He was a young fellow, wearing a gray artillery jacket, with high cavalry boots coming above the knees. I noticed his firm-set jaw, and a pearl-handled revolver stuck carelessly in his belt, but observed no symbol of rank about him.

"Is this Captain Wayne?" he asked, not unpleasantly, I answered by an inclination of the head, and he turned at once toward the others.

"Cass, bring three men over here, and carry this officer to the same wagon you did the others," he commanded briefly. "Fix him comfortably, but be in a hurry about it."

They lifted me in the blanket, one holding tightly at either corner, and bore me tenderly out into the night. Once one of them tripped over a projecting root, and the sudden jar of his stumble shot a spasm of pain through me, which caused me to cry out even through my clinched teeth.

"Pardon me, lads," I panted, ashamed of the weakness, "but it slipped out before I could help it."

"Don't be after a mentionin' av it, yer honor," returned a rich brogue. "Sure an me feet got so mixed oup that I wondher I didn't drap ye entoirely."

"If ye had, Clancy," said the man named Cass, grimly, "I reckon as how the Colonel would have drapped you."

At the foot of a narrow ravine, leading forth into the broader valley, we came to a covered army wagon, to which four mules had been already attached. The canvas was drawn aside, and I was lifted up and carefully deposited in the hay that thickly covered the bottom. It was so intensely dark within I could see nothing of my immediate surroundings, but a low moan told me there must be at

least one other wounded man present. Outside I
heard the tread of horses' hoofs, and then the sound
of Mosby's voice.

"Jake," he said, "drive rapidly, but with as much
care as possible. Take the lower road after you cross
the bridge, and you will meet with no patrols. We
will ride beside you for a couple of miles."

Then a hand thrust aside the canvas, and a face
peered in. I caught a faint glimmer of stars, but could
distinguish little else.

"Boys," said the leader, kindly, "I wish I might
give you better transportation, but this is the only
form of vehicle we can find. I reckon you'll get
pretty badly bumped over the road you are going,
but I'm furnishing you all the chance to get away in
my power."

"For one I am grateful enough," I answered, after
waiting for someone else to speak. "A little pain is
preferable to imprisonment."

"After you pass the bridge you will be perfectly
safe on that score," he said heartily. "Anything more
I can do for any of you?"

"How many of us are there?" asked someone
faintly from out the darkness.

"Oh, yes," returned Mosby, with a laugh, "I forgot; you will want to know each other. There are
three of you—Colonel Colby of North Carolina,
Major Wilkins of Thome's Battery, and Captain
Wayne, ———th Virginia. Let that answer for an

introduction, gentlemen, and now good-night. We shall guard you as long as necessary, and then must leave you to the kindly ministrations of the driver."

He reached in, leaning down from his saddle to do so, drew the blanket somewhat closer about me, and was gone. I caught the words of a sharp, short order, and the heavy wagon lurched forward, its wheels bumping over the irregularities in the road, each jolt sending a fresh spasm of pain through my tortured body.

May the merciful God ever protect me from such a ride again! It seemed interminable, while each long mile we travelled brought with it new and greater agony of mind and body. That I did not suffer alone was early evident from the low moans borne to me from out the darkness. Once a weak, trembling voice prayed for release,—a short, fervent prayer, which so impressed me in the weakness of my own anguish that I added to it "Amen," spoken unconsciously aloud.

"Who spoke?" asked the same voice, faintly.

"I am Captain Wayne," I answered, almost glad to break the terrible silence by speech of any kind; "and I merely echoed your prayer. Death would indeed prove a welcome relief from such intensity of suffering."

"Yes," he acquiesced gently. "I fear I have not sufficient strength to bear mine for long; yet I am a Christian, and there are wife and child waiting for me at home. God knows I am ready when He calls, but my duty is to live, if possible, for their sake. They will have nothing left if I pass on."

"The road must grow smoother as we come down into the valley. Are your wounds serious?"

"I was struck by fragments of a shell," he answered, and I could tell he spoke the words through his clinched teeth, "and am wounded in the head as well as the body—oh, my God!" The cry was wrung from him by a sudden tilting of the wagon, and for a moment my own pain prevented utterance.

"I hear nothing from the other man," I managed to say at last. "Colonel Mosby said there were three of us; surely the third man cannot be already dead?"

"Mercifully unconscious, I think; at least he has made no sound since I was placed in here."

"No, friends," spoke another and deeper voice from farther back within the jolting wagon, "I am not unconscious, but less noticeably in pain. I have lost a leg, yet the stump seems seared and dead, hurting me little unless I touch it."

We lapsed into solemn silence, it was such an effort to talk, and we had so little to say. Each man, no doubt, was struggling, as I know I was, to withhold expression of his agony for the sake of the others. I lay racked in every nerve, my teeth tightly clinched, my temples beaded with perspiration. I could hear the troopers riding without, the jingling of their accoutrements, and the steady beat of their horses' feet being easily distinguishable above the deeper rumble of the wheels. Then there came a quick order in Mosby's familiar voice, a calling aloud of some further directions to the driver, and afterwards nothing was distinguishable excepting the noise of our own rapid progress.

Jake drove, it seemed to me, most recklessly. I could hear the almost constant crack of his lash and the rough words of goading hurled at the straining mules. The road appeared to be filled with roots, while occasionally the wheels would strike a stone, coming down again with a jar that nearly drove me frantic. The chill night air swept in through the open front of the hood, and made me feel as if my veins were filled with ice, even while the inflammation of my wounds burned and throbbed as with fire. The pitiful moaning of the man who lay next me grew gradually fainter, and finally ceased altogether. Tortured as I was, yet I could not but think of the wife and child far away praying for his safe return. For their sake I forced back the intensity of my own sufferings and spoke into the darkness.

"The man who prayed," I said, not knowing which of my two companions it might be. "Are you suffering less, that you have ceased to moan?"

There was no answer. Then the loose hay rustled, as though someone was slowly dragging his helpless body through it. A moment later the deep voice spoke:

"He is dead," solemnly. "God has answered his prayer. His hand already begins to feel cold."

"Dead?" I echoed, inexpressibly shocked. "Do you know his name?"

"As I am Major Wilkins, it must be Colonel Colby who has died. May God be merciful to the widow and the orphan."

The hours that followed were all but endless. I knew we had reached the lower valley, for the road became more level, yet the slightest jolting now was sufficient to render me crazed with pain, and I had lost all power of restraint. My tortured nerves throbbed; the fever gripped me, and my mind began to wander. Visions of delirium came, and I dreamed dreams too terrible for record: demons danced on the drifting clouds before me, while whirling savages chanting in horrid discord stuck my frenzied body full of blazing brands. At times I was awake, calling in vain for water to quench a thirst which grew maddening, then I lapsed into a semi-consciousness that drove me wild with its delirious fancies. I knew vaguely that the Major had crept back through the darkness and passed his strong arm gently beneath my head. I heard him shouting in his deep voice to the driver for something to drink, but was unaware of any response. All became blurred, confused, bewildering. I thought it was my mother comforting me. The faint gray daylight stole in at last through the

cracks of the wagon cover; I could dimly distinguish a dark face bending over me, framed by a
heavy gray beard, and then, merciful unconsciousness came, and I rested as one dead beside the corpse
of the Colonel.

A Woman's Wartime Journal
November 17–22, 1864

[DOLLY SUMNER LUNT]

NOVEMBER 17, 1864

Have been uneasy all day. At night some of the neighbors who had been to town called. They said it was a large force moving very slowly. What shall I do? Where go?

NOVEMBER 18, 1864

Slept very little last night. Went out doors several times and could see large fires like burning buildings. Am I not in the hands of a merciful God who has promised to take care of the widow and orphan?

Sent off two of my mules in the night. Mr. Ward and Frank took them away and hid them. In the morning took a barrel of salt, which had cost me two hundred dollars, into one of the black women's gardens, put a paper over it, and then on the top of that leached ashes. Fixed it on a board as a leach tub, daubing it with ashes. Had some few pieces of meat taken from my smoke-house carried to the Old Place and hidden under some fodder. Bid them hide the wagon and gear and then go on plowing. Went to packing up mine and Sadai's clothes. I fear that we shall be homeless.

The boys came back and wished to hide their mules. They say that the Yankees camped at Mr. Gibson's last night and are taking all the stock in the county. Seeing them so eager, I told them to do as they pleased. They took them off, and Elbert took his forty fattening hogs to the Old Place Swamp and turned them in.

We have done nothing all day—that is, my people have not. I made a pair of pants for Jack. Sent Nute up to Mrs. Perry's on an errand. On his way back, he said, two Yankees met him and begged him to go with them. They asked if we had livestock, and came up the road as far as Mrs. Laura Perry's. I sat for an hour expecting them, but they must have gone back. Oh, how I trust I am safe! Mr. Ward is very much alarmed.

NOVEMBER 19, 1864

Slept in my clothes last night, as I heard that the Yankees went to neighbor Montgomery's on Thursday night at one o'clock, searched his house, drank his wine, and took his money and valuables. As we were not disturbed, I walked after breakfast, with Sadai, up to Mr. Joe Perry's, my nearest neighbor, where the Yankees were yesterday. Saw Mrs. Laura in the road surrounded by her children, seeming to be looking for someone. She said she was looking for her husband, that old Mrs. Perry had just sent her word that the Yankees went to James Perry's the night before, plundered his house, and drove off all his stock, and that she must drive hers into the old fields. Before we were done talking, up came Joe and Jim Perry from their hiding-place. Jim was very much excited. Happening to turn and look behind, as we stood there, I saw some blue-coats coming down the hill. Jim immediately raised his gun, swearing he would kill them anyhow.

"No, don't!" said I, and ran home as fast as I could, with Sadai.

I could hear them cry, "Halt! Halt!" and their guns went off in quick succession. Oh Clod, the time of trial has come!

A man passed on his way to Covington. I hallooed to him, asking him if he did not know the Yankees were coming.

"No—are they?"

"Yes," said I; "they are not three hundred yards from here."

"Sure enough," said he. "Well, I'll not go. I don't want them to get my horse." And although within hearing of their guns, he would stop and look for them. Blissful ignorance! Not knowing, not hearing, he has not suffered the suspense, the fear, that I have for the past forty-eight hours. I walked to the gate. There they came filing up.

I hastened back to my frightened servants and told them that they had better hide, and then went back to the gate to claim protection and a guard. But like demons they rush in! My yards are full. To my smoke-house, my dairy, pantry, kitchen, and cellar, like famished wolves they come, breaking locks and whatever is in their way. The thousand pounds of meat in my smoke-house is gone in a twinkling, my flour, my meat, my lard, butter, eggs, pickles of various kinds—both in vinegar and brine—wine, jars, and jugs are all gone. My eighteen fat turkeys, my hens, chickens, and fowls, my young pigs, are shot down in my yard and hunted as if they were rebels themselves. Utterly powerless I ran out and appealed to the guard.

"I cannot help you, Madam; it is orders."

As I stood there, from my lot I saw driven, first, old Dutch, my dear old buggy horse, who has carried my beloved husband so many miles, and who would so quietly wait at the block for him to mount and dismount, and who at last drew him to his grave; then came old Mary, my brood mare, who for years had been too old and stiff for work, with her three-year-old colt, my two-year-old mule, and her last little baby colt. There they go! There go my mules, my sheep, and, worse than all, my boys!

Alas! little did I think while trying to save my house from plunder and fire that they were forcing my boys from home at the point of the bayonet. One, Newton, jumped into bed in his cabin, and declared himself sick. Another crawled under the floor,—a lame boy he was,—but they pulled him out, placed him on a horse, and drove him off. Mid, poor Mid! The last I saw of him, a man had him going around the garden, looking, as I thought, for my sheep, as he was my shepherd. Jack came crying to me, the big tears coursing down his cheeks, saying they were making him go. I said:

"Stay in my room."

But a man followed in, cursing him and threatening to shoot him if he did not go; so poor Jack had to yield. James Arnold, in trying to escape from a back window, was captured and marched off. Henry, too, was taken; I know not how or when, but probably when he and Bob went after the mules. . . .

My poor boys! My poor boys! What unknown trials are before you! How you have clung to your mistress and assisted her in every way you knew.

Never have I corrected them; a word was sufficient. Never have they known want of any kind. Their parents are with me, and how sadly they lament the loss of their boys. Their cabins are rifled of every valuable, the soldiers swearing that their Sunday clothes were the white people's, and that they never had money to get such things as they had.

Poor Frank's chest was broken open, his money and tobacco taken. He has always been a money-making and saving boy; not infrequently has his crop brought him five hundred dollars and more. All of his clothes and Rachel's clothes, which dear Lou gave before her death and which she had packed away, were stolen from her. Ovens, skillets, coffee-mills, of which we had three, coffee-pots—not one have I left. Sifters all gone!

Seeing that the soldiers could not be restrained, the guard offered me to have their remaining possessions brought into my house, which I did, and they all, poor things, huddled together in my room, fearing every movement that the house would be burned.

A Captain Webber from Illinois came into my house. Of him I claimed protection from the vandals who were forcing themselves into my room. He said that he knew my brother Orrington. At that name I could not restrain my feelings, but, bursting into tears, implored him to see my brother and let him know my destitution. I saw nothing before me but starvation. He promised to do this, and comforted me with the assurance that my dwelling-house would not be burned, though my out-buildings might. Poor little Sadai went crying to him as to a friend and told him that they had taken her doll, Nancy. He begged her to come and see him, and he would give her a fine waxen one.

He felt for me, and I give him and several others the character of gentlemen. I don't believe they would have molested women and children had they had their own way. He seemed surprised that I had not laid away in my house, flour and other provisions. I did not suppose I could secure them there, more than where I usually kept them, for in last summer's raid houses were thoroughly searched. In parting with him; I parted as with a friend.

Sherman himself and a greater portion of his army passed my house that day. All day, as the sad moments rolled on, were they passing not only in front of my house, but from behind; they tore down my garden palings, made a road through my backyard and lot field, driving their stock and riding through, tearing down my fences and desolating my home—wantonly doing it when there was no necessity for it.

Such a day, if I live to the age of Methuselah, may God spare me from ever seeing again!

As night drew its sable curtains around us, the heavens from every point were lit up with flames from burning buildings. Dinnerless and supperless as we were, it was nothing in comparison with the fear of being driven out homeless to the dreary woods. Nothing to eat! I could give my guard no supper, so he left us. I appealed to another, asking him if he had wife, mother, or sister, and how he should feel were they in my situation. A colonel from Vermont left me two men, but they were Dutch, and I could not understand one word they said.

My Heavenly Father alone saved me from the destructive fire. My carriage-house had in it eight bales of cotton, with my carriage, buggy, and harness. On top of the cotton were some carded cotton rolls, a hundred pounds or more. These were thrown out of the blanket in which they were, and a large twist of the rolls taken and set on fire, and thrown into the boat of my carriage, which was close up to the cotton bales. Thanks to my God, the cotton only burned over, and then went out. Shall I ever forget the deliverance?

To-night, when the greater part of the army had passed, it came up very windy and cold. My room was full, nearly, with the negroes and their bedding. They were afraid to go out, for my women could not step out of the door without an insult from the Yankee soldiers. They lay down on the floor; Sadai got down and under the same cover with Sally, while I sat up all night, watching every moment for the flames to burst out from some of my buildings. The two guards came into my room and laid themselves by my fire for the night. I could not close my eyes, but kept walking to and fro, watching the fires in the distance and dreading the approaching day, which, I feared, as they had not all passed, would be but a continuation of horrors.

NOVEMBER 20, 1864

This is the blessed Sabbath, the day upon which He who came to bring peace and good will upon earth rose from His tomb and ascended to intercede for us poor fallen creatures. But how unlike this day to any that have preceded it in my once quiet home. I had watched all night, and the dawn found me watching for the moving of the soldiery that was encamped about us. Oh, how I dreaded those that were to pass, as I supposed they would straggle and complete the ruin that the others had commenced, for I had been repeatedly told that they would burn everything as they passed.

Some of my women had gathered up a chicken that the soldiers shot yesterday, and they cooked it with some yams for our breakfast, the guard complaining that we gave them no supper. They gave us some coffee, which I had to make in a tea-kettle, as every coffeepot is taken off. The rear-guard was commanded by Colonel Carlow, who changed our guard, leaving us one soldier while they were passing. They marched directly on, scarcely breaking ranks. Once a bucket of water was called for, but they drank without coming in.

About ten o'clock they had all passed save one, who came in and wanted coffee made, which was done, and he, too, went on. A few minutes elapsed, and two couriers riding rapidly passed back. Then, presently, more soldiers came by, and this ended the passing of Sherman's army by my place, leaving me poorer by thirty thousand dollars than I was yesterday morning. And a much stronger Rebel!

After the excitement was a little over, I went up to Mrs. Laura's to sympathize with her, for I had no doubt but that her husband was hanged. She thought so, and we could see no way for his escape. We all took a good cry together. While there, I saw smoke looming up in the direction of my home, and thought surely the fiends had done their work ere they left. I ran as fast as I could, but soon saw that the fire was below my home. It proved to be the gin house belonging to Colonel Pitts.

My boys have not come home. I fear they cannot get away from the soldiers. Two of my cows came up this morning, but were driven off again by the Yankees.

I feel so thankful that I have not been burned out that I have tried to spend the remainder of the day as the Sabbath ought to be spent. Ate dinner out of the oven in Julia's house, some stew, no bread. She is boiling some corn. My poor servants feel so badly at losing what they have worked for; meat, the hog meat that they love better than anything else, is all gone.

NOVEMBER 21, 1864

We had the table laid this morning, but no bread or butter or milk. What a prospect for delicacies! My house is a perfect fright. I had brought in Saturday

night some thirty bushels of potatoes and ten or fifteen bushels of wheat poured down on the carpet
in the ell. Then the few gallons of syrup saved was
daubed all about. The backbone of a hog that I
had killed on Friday, and which the Yankees did not
take when they cleaned out my smokehouse, I found
and hid under my bed, and this is all the meat I have.
Major Lee came down this evening, having heard
that I was burned out, to proffer me a home. Mr.
Dorsett was with him. The army lost some of their
beeves in passing. I sent to-day and had some driven
into my lot, and then sent to Judge Glass to come
over and get some. Had two killed. Some of Wheel-
er's men came in, and I asked them to shoot the cattle, which they did.

About ten o'clock this morning Mr. Joe Perry
called. I was so glad to see him that I could scarcely
forbear embracing him. I could not keep from crying, for I was sure the Yankees had executed him,
and I felt so much for his poor wife. The soldiers
told me repeatedly Saturday that they had hung
him and his brother James and George Guise. They
had a narrow escape, however, and only got away by
knowing the country so much better than the soldiers did. They lay out until this morning. How
rejoiced I am for his family! All of his negroes are
gone, save one man that had a wife here at my plantation. They are very strong Secesh. When the army
first came along they offered a guard for the house,

but Mrs. Laura told them she was guarded by a Higher Power, and did not thank them to do it. She says that she could think of nothing else all day when the army was passing but of the devil and his hosts. She had, however, to call for a guard before night or the soldiers would have taken everything she had.

NOVEMBER 22, 1864

After breakfast this morning I went over to my grave-yard to see what had befallen that. To my joy, I found it had not been disturbed. As I stood by my dead, I felt rejoiced that they were at rest. Never have I felt so perfectly reconciled to the death of my husband as I do to-day, while looking upon the ruin of his lifelong labor. How it would have grieved him to see such destruction! Yes, theirs is the lot to be envied. At rest, rest from care, rest from heartaches, from trouble. . . .

Found one of my large hogs killed just outside the grave-yard.

Walked down to the swamp, looking for the wagon and gear that Henry hid before he was taken off. Found some of my sheep; came home very much wearied, having walked over four miles.

Mr. and Mrs. Rockmore called. Major Lee came down again after some cattle, and while he was here the alarm was given that more Yankees were coming. I was terribly alarmed and packed my trunks with clothing, feeling assured that we should be burned out now. Major Lee swore that he would shoot, which frightened me, for he was intoxicated enough to make him ambitious. He rode off in the direction whence it was said they were coming, Soon after, however, he returned, saying it was a false alarm, that it was some of our own men. Oh, dear! Are we to be always living in fear and dread! Oh, the horrors, the horrors of war!

A Grey Sleeve

[STEPHEN CRANE]

I

"It looks as if it might rain this afternoon," remarked the lieutenant of artillery.

"So it does," the infantry captain assented. He glanced casually at the sky. When his eyes had lowered to the green-shadowed landscape before him, he said fretfully: "I wish those fellows out yonder would quit pelting at us. They've been at it since noon."

At the edge of a grove of maples, across wide fields, there occasionally appeared little puffs of smoke of a dull hue in this gloom of sky which expressed an impending rain. The long wave of blue and steel in the field moved uneasily at the eternal barking of the far-away sharpshooters, and the men, leaning upon their rifles, stared at the grove of maples. Once a private turned to borrow some tobacco from a comrade in the rear rank, but, with his hand still stretched out, he continued to twist his head and glance at the distant trees. He was afraid the enemy would shoot him at a time when he was not looking.

Suddenly the artillery officer said: "See what's coming!"

Along the rear of the brigade of infantry a column of cavalry was sweeping at a hard gallop. A lieutenant, riding some yards to the right of the column, bawled furiously at the four troopers just at the rear of the colors. They had lost distance and made a little gap, but at the shouts of the lieutenant they urged their horses forward. The bugler, careering along behind the captain of the troop, fought and tugged like a wrestler to keep his frantic animal from bolting far ahead of the column.

On the springy turf the innumerable hoofs thundered in a swift storm of sound. In the brown faces of the troopers their eyes were set like bits of flashing steel.

The long line of the infantry regiments standing at ease underwent a sudden movement at the rush of the passing squadron. The foot soldiers turned their heads to gaze at the torrent of horses and men.

The yellow folds of the flag fluttered back in silken, shuddering waves, as if it were a reluctant thing. Occasionally a giant spring of a charger would rear the firm and sturdy figure of a soldier suddenly head and shoulders above his comrades. Over the noise of the scudding hoofs could be heard the creaking of leather trappings, the jingle and clank of steel, and the tense, low-toned commands or appeals of the men to their horses; and the horses were mad with the headlong sweep of this movement. Powerful under jaws bent back and straightened, so that the bits were clamped as rigidly as vices upon the teeth, and glistening necks arched in desperate resistance to the hands at the bridles. Swinging their heads in rage at the granite laws of their lives, which compelled even their angers and their ardors to chosen directions and chosen faces, their flight was as a flight of harnessed demons.

The captain's bay kept its pace at the head of the squadron with the lithe bounds of a thoroughbred, and this horse was proud as a chief at the roaring trample of his fellows behind him. The captain's glance was calmly upon the grove of maples whence the sharpshooters of the enemy had been picking at the blue line. He seemed to be reflecting. He stolidly rose and fell with the plunges of his horse in all the indifference of a deacon's figure seated plumply in church. And it occurred to many of the watching infantry to wonder why this officer could remain imperturbable and reflective when his squadron was thundering and swarming behind him like the rushing of a flood.

The column swung in a saber-curve toward a break in a fence, and dashed into a roadway. Once a little plank bridge was encountered, and the sound of the hoofs upon it was like the long roll of many drums. An old captain in the infantry turned to his first lieutenant and made a remark, which was a compound of bitter disparagement of cavalry in general and soldierly admiration of this particular troop.

Suddenly the bugle sounded, and the column halted with a jolting upheaval amid sharp, brief cries. A moment later the men had tumbled from their horses and, carbines in hand, were running in a swarm toward the grove of maples. In the road one of every four of the troopers was standing with braced legs, and pulling and hauling at the bridles of four frenzied horses.

The captain was running awkwardly in his boots. He held his saber low, so that the point often threatened to catch in the turf. His yellow hair ruffled out from under his faded cap. "Go in hard now!" he roared, in a voice of hoarse fury. His face was violently red.

The troopers threw themselves upon the grove like wolves upon a great animal. Along the whole front of woods there was the dry crackling of musketry, with bitter, swift flashes and smoke that writhed like stung phantoms. The troopers yelled shrilly and spanged bullets low into the foliage.

For a moment, when near the woods, the line almost halted. The men struggled and fought for a time like swimmers encountering a powerful current. Then with a supreme effort they went on again. They dashed madly at the grove, whose foliage from the high light of the field was as inscrutable as a wall.

Then suddenly each detail of the calm trees became apparent, and with a few more frantic leaps the men were in the cool gloom of the woods. There was a heavy odor as from burned paper. Wisps of grey smoke wound upward. The men halted and, grimy, perspiring, and puffing, they searched the recesses of the woods with eager, fierce glances. Figures could be seen flitting afar off. A dozen carbines rattled at them in an angry volley.

During this pause the captain strode along the line, his face lit with a broad smile of contentment. "When he sends this crowd to do anything, I guess he'll find we do it pretty sharp," he said to the grinning lieutenant.

"Say, they didn't stand that rush a minute, did they?" said the subaltern. Both officers were profoundly dusty in their uniforms, and their faces were soiled like those of two urchins.

Out in the grass behind them were three tumbled and silent forms.

Presently the line moved forward again. The men went from tree to tree like hunters stalking game. Some at the left of the line fired occasionally, and those at the right gazed curiously in that direction. The men still breathed heavily from their scramble across the field.

Of a sudden a trooper halted and said: "Hello! there's a house!" Every one paused. The men turned to look at their leader.

The captain stretched his neck and swung his head from side to side. "By George, it is a house!" he said.

Through the wealth of leaves there vaguely loomed the form of a large white house. These troopers, brown-faced from many days of campaigning, each feature of them telling of their placid confidence and courage, were stopped abruptly by the appearance of this house. There was some subtle suggestion—some tale of an unknown thing—which watched them from they knew not what part of it.

A rail fence girded a wide lawn of tangled grass. Seven pines stood along a drive-way which led from two distant posts of a vanished gate. The blue-clothed troopers moved forward until they stood at the fence peering over it.

The captain put one hand on the top rail and seemed to be about to climb the fence, when suddenly he hesitated, and said in a low voice: "Watson, what do you think of it?"

The lieutenant stared at the house. "Derned if I know!" he replied.

The captain pondered. It happened that the whole company had turned a gaze of profound awe and doubt upon this edifice which confronted them. The men were very silent.

At last the captain swore and said: "We are certainly a pack of fools. Derned old deserted house halting a company of Union cavalry, and making us gape like babies!"

"Yes, but there's something—something—" insisted the subaltern in a half stammer.

"Well, if there's 'something—something' in there, I'll get it out," said the captain. "Send Sharpe clean around to the other side with about twelve men, so we will sure bag your 'something—something,' and I'll take a few of the boys and find out what's in the d——d old thing!"

He chose the nearest eight men for his "storming party," as the lieutenant called it. After he had waited some minutes for the others to get into position, he said "Come ahead" to his eight men, and climbed the fence.

The brighter light of the tangled lawn made him suddenly feel tremendously apparent, and he wondered if there could be some mystic thing in the house which was regarding this approach. His men trudged silently at his back. They stared at the windows and lost themselves in deep speculations as to the probability of there being, perhaps, eyes behind the blinds—malignant eyes, piercing eyes.

Suddenly a corporal in the party gave vent to a startled exclamation, and half threw his carbine into position. The captain turned quickly, and the corporal said: "I saw an arm move the blinds—an arm with a grey sleeve!"

"Don't be a fool, Jones, now," said the captain sharply.

"I swear t'—" began the corporal, but the captain silenced him.

When they arrived at the front of the house, the troopers paused, while the captain went softly up the front steps. He stood before the large front door and studied it. Some crickets chirped in the long grass, and the nearest pine could be heard in its endless sighs. One of the privates moved uneasily, and his foot crunched the gravel. Suddenly the captain swore angrily and kicked the door with a loud crash. It flew open.

II

The bright lights of the day flashed into the old house when the captain angrily kicked open the door. He was aware of a wide hallway, carpeted with matting and extending deep into the dwelling. There was also an old walnut hat-rack and a little marble-topped table with a vase and two books upon it. Farther back was a great, venerable fireplace containing dreary ashes.

But directly in front of the captain was a young girl. The flying open of the door had obviously been an utter astonishment to her, and she remained transfixed there in the middle of the floor, staring at the captain with wide eyes.

She was like a child caught at the time of a raid upon the cake. She wavered to and fro upon her feet, and held her hands behind her. There were two little points of terror in her eyes, as she gazed up at the young captain in dusty blue, with his reddish, bronze complexion, his yellow hair, his bright saber held threateningly.

These two remained motionless and silent, simply staring at each other for some moments.

The captain felt his rage fade out of him and leave his mind limp. He had been violently angry, because this house had made him feel hesitant, wary. He did not like to be wary. He liked to feel confident, sure. So he had kicked the door open, and had been prepared, to march in like a soldier of wrath.

But now he began, for one thing, to wonder if his uniform was so dusty and old in appearance. Moreover, he had a feeling that his face was covered with a compound of dust, grime, and perspiration. He took a step forward and said: "I didn't mean to frighten you." But his voice was coarse from his battle-howling. It seemed to him to have hempen fibers in it.

The girl's breath came in little, quick gasps, and she looked at him as she would have looked at a serpent.

"I didn't mean to frighten you," he said again.

The girl, still with her hands behind her, began to back away.

"Is there any one else in the house?" he went on, while slowly following her. "I don't wish to disturb you, but we had a fight with some rebel skirmishers in the woods, and I thought maybe some of them might have come in here. In fact, I was pretty sure of it. Are there any of them here?"

The girl looked at him and said, "No!" He wondered why extreme agitation made the eyes of some women so limpid and bright.

"Who is here besides yourself?"

By this time his pursuit had driven her to the end of the hall, and she remained there with her back to the wall and her hands still behind her. When she answered this question, she did not look at him but down at the floor. She cleared her voice and then said: "There is no one here."

"No one?"

She lifted her eyes to him in that appeal that the human being must make even to falling trees, crashing boulders, the sea in a storm, and said, "No, no, there is no one here." He could plainly see her tremble.

Of a sudden he bethought him that she continually kept her hands behind her. As he recalled her air when first discovered, he remembered she appeared precisely as a child detected at one of the crimes of childhood. Moreover, she had always backed away from him. He thought now that she was concealing something which was an evidence of the presence of the enemy in the house.

"What are you holding behind you?" he said suddenly.

She gave a little quick moan, as if some grim hand had throttled her.

"What are you holding behind you?"

"Oh, nothing—please. I am not holding anything behind me; indeed I'm not."

"Very well. Hold your hands out in front of you, then."

"Oh, indeed, I'm not holding anything behind me. Indeed I'm not."

"Well," he began. Then he paused, and remained for a moment dubious. Finally, he laughed. "Well, I shall have my men search the house, anyhow. I'm sorry to trouble you, but I feel sure that there is some—one here whom we want." He turned to the corpo-ral, who with the other men was gaping quietly in at the door, and said: "Jones, go through the house."

As for himself, he remained planted in front of the girl, for she evidently did not dare to move and allow him to see what she held so carefully behind her back. So she was his prisoner.

The men rummaged around on the ground floor of the house. Sometimes the captain called to them, "Try that closet," "Is there any cellar?" But they found no one, and at last they went trooping toward the stairs which led to the second floor.

But at this movement on the part of the men the girl uttered a cry—a cry of such fright and appeal that the men paused. "Oh, don't go up there! Please don't go up there!—ple-ease! There is no one there! Indeed—indeed there is not! Oh, ple-ease!"

"Go on, Jones," said the captain calmly.

The obedient corporal made a preliminary step, and the girl bounded toward the stairs with another cry.

As she passed him, the captain caught sight of that which she had concealed behind her back, and which she had forgotten in this supreme moment. It was a pistol.

She ran to the first step, and standing there, faced the men, one hand extended with perpendicular palm, and the other holding the pistol at her side. "Oh, please, don't go up there! Nobody is there— indeed, there is not! *P-l-e-a-s-e!*" Then suddenly she sank swiftly down upon the step, and, huddling forlornly, began to weep in the agony and with the convulsive tremors of an infant. The pistol fell from her fingers and rattled down to the floor.

The astonished troopers looked at their astonished captain. There was a short silence.

Finally, the captain stooped and picked up the pistol. It was a heavy weapon of the army pattern. He ascertained that it was empty.

He leaned toward the shaking girl, and said gently: "Will you tell me what you were going to do with this pistol?"

He had to repeat the question a number of times, but at last a muffled voice said, "Nothing."

"Nothing!" He insisted quietly upon a further answer. At the tender tones of the captain's voice, the phlegmatic corporal turned and winked gravely at the man next to him.

"Won't you tell me?"

The girl shook her head.

"Please tell me!"

The silent privates were moving their feet uneasily and wondering how long they were to wait.

The captain said: "Please, won't you tell me?"

Then this girl's voice began in stricken tones half coherent, and amid violent sobbing: "It was grandpa's. He—he—he said he was going to shoot anybody who came in here—he didn't care if there were thousands of 'em. And—and I know he would, and I was afraid they'd kill him. And so—and—so I stole away his pistol—and I was going to hide it when you—you—you kicked open the door."

The men straightened up and looked at each other. The girl began to weep again.

The captain mopped his brow. He peered down at the girl. He mopped his brow again. Suddenly he said: "Ah, don't cry like that."

He moved restlessly and looked down at his boots. He mopped his brow again.

Then he gripped the corporal by the arm and dragged him some yards back from the others. "Jones," he said, in an intensely earnest voice, "will you tell me what in the devil I am going to do?"

The corporal's countenance became illuminated with satisfaction at being thus requested to advise his superior officer. He adopted an air of great thought, and finally said: "Well, of course, the feller with the grey sleeve must be upstairs, and we must get past the girl and up there somehow. Suppose I take her by the arm and lead her——"

"What!" interrupted the captain from between his clinched teeth. As he turned away from the corporal, he said fiercely over his shoulder: "You touch that girl and I'll split your skull!"

III

The corporal looked after his captain with an expression of mingled amazement, grief, and philosophy. He seemed to be saying to himself that there unfortunately were times, after all, when one could not rely upon the most reliable of men. When he returned to the group he found the captain bending over the girl and saying: "Why is it that you don't want us to search upstairs?"

The girl's head was buried in her crossed arms. Locks of her hair had escaped from their fastenings, and these fell upon her shoulder.

"Won't you tell me?"

The corporal here winked again at the man next to him.

"Because," the girl moaned, "because—there isn't anybody up there."

The captain at last said timidly: "Well, I'm afraid—
I'm afraid we'll have to—"

The girl sprang to her feet again, and implored
him with her hands. She looked deep into his eyes
with her glance, which was at this time like that of
the fawn when it says to the hunter, "Have mercy
upon me!"

These two stood regarding each other. The captain's foot was on the bottom step, but he seemed
to be shrinking. He wore an air of being deeply
wretched and ashamed. There was a silence!

Suddenly the corporal said in a quick, low tone:
"Look out, captain!"

All turned their eyes swiftly toward the head of
the stairs. There had appeared there a youth in a grey
uniform. He stood looking coolly down at them.
No word was said by the troopers. The girl gave vent
to a little wail of desolation, "O Harry!"

He began slowly to descend the stairs. His right
arm was in a white sling, and there were some fresh
blood-stains upon the cloth. His face was rigid and
deathly pale, but his eyes flashed like lights. The
girl was again moaning in an utterly dreary fashion,
as the youth came slowly down toward the silent
men in blue.

Six steps from the bottom of the flight he halted
and said: "I reckon it's me you're looking for."

The troopers had crowded forward a trifle and,
posed in lithe, nervous attitudes, were watching him

like cats. The captain remained unmoved. At the youth's question he merely nodded his head and said, "Yes."

The young man in grey looked down at the girl, and then, in the same even tone which now, however, seemed to vibrate with suppressed fury, he said: "And is that any reason why you should insult my sister?"

At this sentence, the girl intervened, desperately, between the young man in grey and the officer in blue. "Oh, don't, Harry, don't! He was good to me! He was good to me, Harry—indeed he was!"

The youth came on in his quiet, erect fashion, until the girl could have touched either of the men with her hand, for the captain still remained with his foot upon the first step. She continually repeated: "O Harry! O Harry!"

The youth in grey maneuvered to glare into the captain's face, first over one shoulder of the girl and then over the other. In a voice that rang like metal, he said: "You are armed and unwounded, while I have no weapons and am wounded; but—"

The captain had stepped back and sheathed his saber. The eyes of these two men were gleaming fire, but otherwise the captain's countenance was imperturbable. He said: "You are mistaken. You have no reason to—"

"You lie!"

All save the captain and the youth in grey started in an electric movement. These two words crackled in the air like shattered glass. There was a breathless silence.

The captain cleared his throat. His look at the youth contained a quality of singular and terrible ferocity, but he said in his stolid tone: "I don't suppose you mean what you say now."

Upon his arm he had felt the pressure of some unconscious little fingers. The girl was leaning against the wall as if she no longer knew how to keep her balance, but those fingers—he held his arm very still. She murmured: "O Harry, don't! He was good to me—indeed he was!"

The corporal had come forward until he in a measure confronted the youth in grey, for he saw those fingers upon the captain's arm, and he knew that sometimes very strong men were not able to move hand nor foot under such conditions.

The youth had suddenly seemed to become weak. He breathed heavily and clung to the rail. He was glaring at the captain, and apparently summoning all his will power to combat his weakness. The corporal addressed him with profound straightforwardness: "Don't you be a derned fool!" The youth turned toward him so fiercely that the corporal threw up a knee and an elbow like a boy who expects to be cuffed.

The girl pleaded with the captain. "You won't hurt him, will you? He don't know what he's saying. He's wounded, you know. Please don't mind him!"

"I won't touch him," said the captain, with rather extraordinary earnestness; "don't you worry about him at all. I won't touch him!"

Then he looked at her, and the girl suddenly withdrew her fingers from his arm.

The corporal contemplated the top of the stairs, and remarked without surprise: "There's another of 'em coming!"

An old man was clambering down the stairs with much speed. He waved a cane wildly. "Get out of my house, you thieves! Get out! I won't have you cross my threshold! Get out!" He mumbled and wagged his head in an old man's fury. It was plainly his intention to assault them.

And so it occurred that a young girl became engaged in protecting a stalwart captain, fully armed, and with eight grim troopers at his back, from the attack of an old man with a walking-stick!

A blush passed over the temples and brow of the captain, and he looked particularly savage and weary. Despite the girl's efforts, he suddenly faced the old man.

"Look here," he said distinctly, "we came in because we had been fighting in the woods yonder, and we concluded that some of the enemy were in this house, especially when we saw a grey sleeve at the window. But this young man is wounded, and I have nothing to say to him. I will even take it for granted that there are no others like him upstairs. We will go away, leaving your d——d old house just as we found it! And we are no more thieves and rascals than you are!"

The old man simply roared: "I haven't got a cow nor a pig nor a chicken on the place! Your soldiers have stolen everything they could carry away. They have torn down half my fences for firewood. This afternoon some of your accursed bullets even broke my window panes!"

The girl had been faltering: "Grandpa! O grandpa!"

The captain looked at the girl. She returned his glance from the shadow of the old man's shoulder. After studying her face a moment, he said: "Well, we will go now." He strode toward the door, and his men clanked docilely after him.

At this time there was the sound of harsh cries and rushing footsteps from without. The door flew open, and a whirlwind composed of blue-coated troopers came in with a swoop. It was headed by the lieutenant. "Oh, here you are!" he cried, catching his breath. "We thought—Oh, look at the girl!"

The captain said intensely: "Shut up, you fool!"

The men settled to a halt with a clash and a bang. There could be heard the dulled sound of many hoofs outside of the house.

"Did you order up the horses?" inquired the captain.

"Yes. We thought——"

"Well, then, let's get out of here," interrupted the captain morosely.

The men began to filter out into the open air. The youth in grey had been hanging dismally to the railing of the stairway. He now was climbing slowly up to the second floor. The old man was addressing himself directly to the serene corporal.

"Not a chicken on the place!" he cried.

"Well, I didn't take your chickens, did I?"

"No, maybe you didn't, but——"

The captain crossed the hall and stood before the girl in rather a culprit's fashion. "You are not angry at me, are you?" he asked timidly.

"No," she said. She hesitated a moment, and then suddenly held out her hand. "You were good to me—and I'm—much obliged."

The captain took her hand, and then he blushed, for he found himself unable to formulate a sentence that applied in any way to the situation.

She did not seem to heed that hand for a time.

He loosened his grasp presently, for he was ashamed to hold it so long without saying anything clever. At last, with an air of charging an entrenched brigade, he contrived to say: "I would rather do anything than frighten or trouble you."

His brow was warmly perspiring. He had a sense of being hideous in his dusty uniform and with his grimy face.

She said, "Oh, I'm so glad it was you instead of somebody who might have—might have hurt brother Harry and grandpa!"

He told her, "I wouldn't have hurt 'em for anything!"

There was a little silence.

"Well, good-bye!" he said at last.

"Good-bye!"

He walked toward the door past the old man, who was scolding at the vanishing figure of the corporal. The captain looked back. She had remained there watching him.

At the bugle's order, the troopers standing beside their horses swung briskly into the saddle. The lieutenant said to the first sergeant:

"Williams, did they ever meet before?"

"Hanged if I know!"

"Well, say—"

The captain saw a curtain move at one of the windows. He cantered from his position at the head of the column and steered his horse between two flower-beds.

"Well, good-bye!"

The squadron trampled slowly past.

"Good-bye!"

They shook hands.

He evidently had something enormously important to say to her, but it seems that he could not manage it. He struggled heroically. The bay charger, with his great mystically solemn eyes, looked around the corner of his shoulder at the girl.

The captain studied a pine tree. The girl inspected the grass beneath the window. The captain said hoarsely: "I don't suppose—I don't suppose—I'll ever see you again!"

She looked at him affrightedly and shrank back from the window. He seemed to have woefully expected a reception of this kind for his question. He gave her instantly a glance of appeal.

She said: "Why, no, I don't suppose you will."

"Never?"

"Why, no, 'tain't possible. You—you are a—Yankee!"

"Oh, I know it, but—" Eventually he continued: "Well, some day, you know, when there's no more fighting, we might—" He observed that she had again withdrawn suddenly into the shadow, so he said: "Well, good-bye!"

When he held her fingers she bowed her head, and he saw a pink blush steal over the curves of her cheek and neck.

"Am I never going to see you again?"

She made no reply.

"Never?" he repeated.

After a long time, he bent over to hear a faint reply: "Sometimes—when there are no troops in the neighborhood—grandpa don't mind if I—walk over as far as that old oak tree yonder—in the afternoons."

It appeared that the captain's grip was very strong, for she uttered an exclamation and looked at her fingers as if she expected to find them mere fragments. He rode away.

The bay horse leaped a flowerbed. They were almost to the drive, when the girl uttered a panic-stricken cry.

The captain wheeled his horse violently, and upon his return journey went straight through a flowerbed.

The girl had clasped her hands. She beseeched him wildly with her eyes. "Oh, please, don't believe it! I never walk to the old oak tree. Indeed I don't! I never—never—never walk there."

The bridle drooped on the bay charger's neck. The captain's figure seemed limp. With an expression of profound dejection and gloom he stared off at where the leaden sky met the dark green line of the woods. The long-impending rain began to fall with a mournful patter, drop and drop. There was a silence.

At last a low voice said, "Well—I might—sometimes I might—perhaps—but only once in a great while—I might walk to the old tree—in the afternoons."

A Horseman in the Sky

[AMBROSE BIERCE]

CHAPTER I

One sunny afternoon in the autumn of the year 1861 a soldier lay in a clump of laurel by the side of a road in western Virginia. He lay at full length upon his stomach, his feet resting upon the toes, his head upon the left forearm. His extended right hand loosely grasped his rifle. But for the somewhat methodical disposition of his limbs and a slight rhythmic movement of the cartridge-box at the back of his belt he might have been thought to be dead. He was asleep at his post of duty. But if detected he would be dead shortly afterward, death being the just and legal penalty of his crime.

The clump of laurel in which the criminal lay was in the angle of a road which after ascending southward a steep acclivity to that point turned sharply to the west, running on the summit for perhaps one hundred yards. There it turned southward again and went zigzagging downward through the forest. At the salient of that second angle was a large flat rock, jutting out northward, overlooking the deep valley from which the road ascended. The rock capped a high cliff; a stone dropped from its outer edge would have fallen sheer downward one thousand feet to the tops of the pines. The angle where the soldier lay was on another spur of the same cliff. Had he been awake he would have commanded a view, not only of the short arm of the road and the jutting rock, but of the entire profile of the cliff below it. It might well have made him giddy to look.

The country was wooded everywhere except at the bottom of the valley to the northward, where there was a small natural meadow, through which flowed a stream scarcely visible from the valley's rim. This open ground looked hardly larger than an ordinary door-yard, but was really several acres in extent. Its green was more vivid than that of the enclosing forest. Away beyond it rose a line of giant cliffs similar to those upon which we are supposed to stand in our survey of the savage scene, and through which the road had somehow made its climb to the summit. The configuration of the valley, indeed, was such that from this point of observation it seemed entirely shut in, and one could but have wondered how the road which found a way out of it had found a way into it, and whence came and whither went the waters of the stream that parted the meadow more than a thousand feet below.

No country is so wild and difficult but men will make it a theatre of war; concealed in the forest at the bottom of that military rat-trap, in which half a hundred men in possession of the exits might have starved an army to submission, lay five regiments of Federal infantry. They had marched all the previous day and night and were resting. At nightfall they would take to the road again, climb to the place where their unfaithful sentinel now slept, and descending the other slope of the ridge fall upon a camp of the enemy at about midnight. Their hope was to surprise it, for the road led to the rear of it. In case of failure, their position would be perilous in the extreme; and fall they surely would should accident or vigilance apprise the enemy of the movement.

CHAPTER II

The sleeping sentinel in the clump of laurel was a young Virginian named Carter Druse. He was the son of wealthy parents, an only child, and had known such ease and cultivation and high living as wealth and taste were able to command in the mountain country of western Virginia. His home was but a few miles from where he now lay. One morning he had risen from the breakfast-table and said, quietly but gravely: "Father, a Union regiment has arrived at Grafton. I am going to join it."

The father lifted his leonine head, looked at the son a moment in silence, and replied: "Well, go, sir, and whatever may occur do what you conceive to be your duty. Virginia, to which you are a traitor, must get on without you. Should we both live to the end of the war, we will speak further of the matter. Your mother, as the physician has informed you, is in a most critical condition; at the best she cannot be with us longer than a few weeks, but that time is precious. It would be better not to disturb her."

So Carter Druse, bowing reverently to his father, who returned the salute with a stately courtesy that masked a breaking heart, left the home of his childhood to go soldiering. By conscience and courage, by deeds of devotion and daring, he soon commended himself to his fellows and his officers; and it was to these qualities and to some knowledge of the country that he owed his selection for his present perilous duty at the extreme outpost. Nevertheless, fatigue had been stronger than resolution and he had fallen asleep. What good or bad angel came in a dream to rouse him from his state of crime, who shall say? Without a movement, without a sound, in the profound silence and the languor of the late afternoon, some invisible messenger of fate touched with unsealing finger the eyes of his consciousness— whispered into the ear of his spirit the mysterious awakening word which no human lips ever have spoken, no human memory ever has recalled. He quietly raised his forehead from his arm and looked between the masking stems of the laurels, instinctively closing his right hand about the stock of his rifle.

His first feeling was a keen artistic delight. On a colossal pedestal, the cliff,—motionless at the extreme edge of the capping rock and sharply outlined against the sky,—was an equestrian statue of impressive dignity. The figure of the man sat the figure of the horse, straight and soldierly, but with the repose of a Grecian god carved in the marble which limits the suggestion of activity. The gray costume harmonized with its aerial background; the metal of accoutrement and caparison was softened and subdued by the shadow; the animal's skin had no points of high light. A carbine strikingly foreshortened lay across the pommel of the saddle, kept in place by the right hand grasping it at the "grip"; the left hand, holding the bridle rein, was invisible. In silhouette against the sky the profile of the horse was cut with the sharpness of a cameo; it looked across the heights of air to the confronting cliffs beyond. The face of the rider, turned slightly away, showed only an outline of temple and beard; lie was looking downward to the bottom of the valley. Magnified by its lift against the sky and by the soldier's testifying sense of the formidableness of a near enemy the group appeared of heroic, almost colossal, size.

For an instant Druse had a strange, half-defined feeling that he had slept to the end of the war and was looking upon a noble work of art reared upon that eminence to commemorate the deeds of an heroic past of which he had been an inglorious part. The feeling was dispelled by a slight movement of the group: the horse, without moving its feet, had drawn its body slightly backward from the verge; the man remained immobile as before. Broad awake and keenly alive to the significance of the situation, Druse now brought the butt of his rifle against his cheek by cautiously pushing the barrel forward through the bushes, cocked the piece, and glancing through the sights covered a vital spot of the horseman's breast. A touch upon the trigger and all would have been well with Carter Druse. At that instant the horseman turned his head and looked in the direction of his concealed foeman—seemed to look into his very face, into his eyes, into his brave, compassionate heart.

Is it then so terrible to kill an enemy in war—an enemy who has surprised a secret vital to the safety of one's self and comrades—an enemy more formidable for his knowledge than all his army for its numbers? Carter Druse grew pale; he shook in every limb, turned faint, and saw the statuesque group before him as black figures, rising, falling, moving unsteadily in arcs of circles in a fiery sky. His hand fell away from his weapon, his head slowly dropped until his face rested on the leaves in which he lay. This courageous gentleman and hardy soldier was near swooning from intensity of emotion.

It was not for long; in another moment his face was raised from earth, his hands resumed their places on the rifle, his forefinger sought the trigger; mind, heart, and eyes were clear, conscience and reason sound. He could not hope to capture that enemy; to alarm him would but send him dashing to his camp with his fatal news. The duty of the soldier was plain: the man must be shot dead from ambush—without warning, without a moment's spiritual preparation, with never so much as an unspoken prayer, he must be sent to his account. But no—there is a hope; he may have discovered nothing—perhaps he is but admiring the sublimity of the landscape. If permitted, he may turn and ride carelessly away in the direction whence he came. Surely it will be possible to judge at the instant of his withdrawing whether he knows. It may well be that his fixity of attention—Druse turned his head and looked through the deeps of air downward, as from the surface to the bottom of a translucent sea. He saw creeping across the green meadow a sinuous line of figures of men and horses— some foolish commander was permitting the soldiers of his escort to water their beasts in the open, in plain view from a dozen summits!

Druse withdrew his eyes from the valley and fixed them again upon the group of man and horse in the sky, and again it was through the sights of his rifle. But this time his aim was at the horse. In his memory, as if they were a divine mandate, rang the words of his father at their parting: "Whatever may occur, do what you conceive to be your duty." He was calm now. His teeth were firmly but not rigidly closed; his nerves were as tranquil as a sleeping babe's—not a tremor affected any muscle of his body; his breathing, until suspended in the act of taking aim, was regular and slow. Duty had conquered; the spirit had said to the body: "Peace, be still." He fired.

CHAPTER III

An officer of the Federal force, who in a spirit of adventure or in quest of knowledge had left the hidden bivouac in the valley, and with aimless feet had made his way to the lower edge of a small open space near the foot of the cliff, was considering what he had to gain by pushing his exploration further. At a distance of a quarter-mile before him, but apparently at a stone's throw, rose from its fringe of pines the gigantic face of rock, towering to so great a height above him that it made him giddy to look up to where its edge cut a sharp, rugged line against the sky. It presented a clean, vertical profile against a background of blue sky to a point half the way down, and of distant hills, hardly less blue, thence to the tops of the trees at its base. Lifting his eyes to the dizzy altitude of its summit the officer saw an astonishing sight—a man on horseback riding down into the valley through the air!

Straight upright sat the rider, in military fashion, with a firm seat in the saddle, a strong clutch upon the rein to hold his charger from too impetuous a plunge. From his bare head his long hair streamed upward, waving like a plume. His hands were concealed in the cloud of the horse's lifted mane. The animal's body was as level as if every hoof-stroke encountered the resistant earth. Its motions were those of a wild gallop, but even as the officer looked they ceased, with all the legs thrown sharply forward as in the act of alighting from a leap. But this was a flight!

Filled with amazement and terror by this apparition of a horseman in the sky—half believing himself the chosen scribe of some new Apocalypse, the officer was overcome by the intensity of his emotions; his legs failed him and he fell. Almost at the same instant he heard a crashing sound in the trees— a sound that died without an echo—and all was still.

The officer rose to his feet, trembling. The familiar sensation of an abraded shin recalled his dazed faculties. Pulling himself together he ran rapidly obliquely away from the cliff to a point distant from its foot; thereabout he expected to find his man; and thereabout he naturally failed. In the fleeting instant of his vision his imagination had been so wrought upon by the apparent grace and ease and intention of the marvelous performance that it did not occur to him that the line of march of aerial cavalry is directly downward, and that he could find the objects of his search at the very foot of the cliff. A half-hour later he returned to camp.

This officer was a wise man; he knew better than to tell an incredible truth. He said nothing of what he had seen. But when the commander asked him if in his scout he had learned anything of advantage to the expedition he answered:

"Yes, sir; there is no road leading down into this valley from the southward."

The commander, knowing better, smiled.

CHAPTER IV

After firing his shot, Private Carter Druse reloaded his rifle and resumed his watch. Ten minutes had hardly passed when a Federal sergeant crept cautiously to him on hands and knees. Druse neither turned his head nor looked at him, but lay without motion or sign of recognition.

"Did you fire?" the sergeant whispered.

"Yes."

"At what?"

"A horse. It was standing on yonder rock—pretty far out. You see it is no longer there. It went over the cliff."

The man's face was white, but he showed no other sign of emotion. Having answered, he turned away his eyes and said no more. The sergeant did not understand.

"See here, Druse," he said, after a moment's silence, "it's no use making a mystery. I order you to report. Was there anybody on the horse?"

"Yes."

"Well?"

"My father."

The sergeant rose to his feet and walked away. "Good God!" he said.

The Last Shot

All through the day, since at first streak of
dawn, the signal-gun had sent its grim,
hoarse challenge down the silent lines, the
thunder of a thousand cannon had mingled with the
ceaseless rattle of musketry to create din infernal.

From the sulphurous vapor, which hangs like a
gray pall about the crest of the hills, sweeps forth,
now here, now there, a dense roll of smoke pierced by
a sullen flame—a roar that makes the solid earth
tremble; and through the air comes the screaming
messenger of death, to fall among the toiling gunners
to the right or to the left, to vanish in a cloud of
smoke, leaving to those around but the memory of
brave comrades gone—to desolate homes far away, but
the canker of a lasting sorrow. Such is war. Such, a soldier's death.

The young Federal artilleryman who stood with thumb on vent, facing the hurtling shower of death, almost unconscious of its import, had risen with the first warning note of action to tireless service at his gun. So weary was the frame, so blunted the sensibilities, from incessant labor, that his duties were performed mechanically, almost without volition, while his whole attention was fixed on a spot directly across the valley, where an occasional rift in the cloud of smoke revealed the position of a Confederate battery and (what especially riveted his attention) a gunner, "number three," like himself, attached to a piece on the left of the line, and whose object seemed to be to silence the gun which the young Federal soldier was serving.

A gleam of ferocity shone out for a moment from the grimy face of the boy in blue, as a shell tore a great hole in the earth a little to the right of him, scattering death all around.

Slightly changing the position of his gun so as to bear directly upon the Confederate piece, for he was gunner as well as "number three," on that memorable day, a day when Battery B was unofficered by death, the artilleryman trained "Destroyer" carefully upon his annoying adversary, and the shell was sent shrieking on its way.

"Too short," muttered "number three," as the messenger was seen to plow a furrow in the hillside in front of the Confederates and richochet over their heads to explode in the woods behind.

Puff—and a demoniac return from the Confederates tore off the top of the sapling not ten yards away.

Again the Federal gun was trained upon the Confederate "number three," for the tall figures of both artillerymen could be distinctly seen across the narrow valley, and the erect form between the wheels became the target of each. This time the iron messenger tore through a veil of smoke that wafted over a battery on the right, and its effect could not be seen; but the response was almost immediate, and as the shell buried itself in the earth and exploded a few yards in advance to the left, "number one" staggered to the rear, badly hurt. The eyes of the young Federal fairly blazed.

"Cut that fuse a little shorter," he shouted. "We'll explode it in his face this time."

On sped the fateful iron—Ah!—Ere it reaches the grim muzzle of the Confederate gun—a flash—and "number two" is seen to grasp at a wheel for support as he sinks to the ground, while an officer's horse drops in his tracks, carrying the rider with him.

A shout goes up from the tired men who seem now to be endowed with new life. But alas! two of them shout for the last time. The compliment is returned with interest, killing numbers two and five, and tearing a gun-wheel to pieces, necessitating a delay of ten minutes to adjust a new one. The Confederate waited in silence, letting his gun cool until the next shot from the Federals tore along through the lines, cutting up a great deal of dirt but doing no damage, when he responded, killing a horse and dismounting an ammunition caisson.

By this time both combatants were lost to all thought of what was going on about them, save the service of their pieces. From a wooded hillock about two hundred yards to the left a detachment of sharpshooters had found lodgment, who poured in an incessant fire upon the Federals. Their leaden messengers whistled constantly past the duelist in blue, now burying themselves in the woodwork of the gun-carriage, now splintering the spokes of the wheels, or flattening themselves with a vicious thud against the metal itself. Had it not been for the heavy curtain of smoke enveloping the batteries on the left and slightly in advance, he would certainly have been killed. It was seldom, however, that this curtain lifted sufficiently to reveal him to his enemies, who could only direct their fire at the lurid gleams of light piercing the cloud at every discharge of the cannon, and so locating the position of the men. Directly in front of the Federal, however, and around and about the small knoll upon which his Confederate *vis-a-vis* had planted his gun, for some reason the cloud, which enveloped both ridges and frequently swept down the sloping sides of the hills, had not settled; so that the effect of each shot could be noted and the fire directed with such accuracy as the gunners might exercise—a question of skill, of superiority of ordnance and marksmanship. There had been no cessation, no rest. Yet now that an hour of light remained,—now that the sun hung like a great globe of blood just above the horizon,—the labor of the day was as naught, wounds were nothing. The gray artilleryman, still unconquered, waves a sarcastic defiance as he sends once more his hurtling challenge.

Again and again the cannon belched forth their angry flame. Again and again the screaming shells burst in and around the blackened fiends about the guns. Only three remained to man the grim "Destroyer"— *only three;* the others are scattered here and there, where they had fallen. The slackened fire from the Confederate side told an awful tale. Yet did these two demons of destruction stand face to face, unscathed, unconquered—the blue and the gray—erect, clear-outlined against the dark bordering of the forest behind them, as the great red sun sank down behind the hilltops.

"Once more ere the night is here!" cried the blue.

"Once more while daylight lasts!" cried the gray.

In mid air the last shots hissed past each other as they sped upon their deadly errand.

For a moment it seemed as though the earth had opened, emitting a scorching tongue of flame, which shot from hell to heaven, and—it was gone—and so were all the blue save "number three," who, crawling from beneath the splintered carriage, struggled forward and scanned with eager gaze the opposite hilltop, where a tall form was seen to totter and fall amid the wreckage of a gun. With a last supreme effort the dying soldier seized the ragged, shot-torn guidon, waving it defiantly, as he feebly gasped a faint "Hurrah!"—then came night and darkness—and rest. For the dead heroes, rest eternal; for the survivors, the sleep of utter exhaustion, dreamless and undisturbed even by ghastly reminders of the day's fierce struggle. On the morrow these will wake to glory—glory surpassing, abounding; piercing the clouds of smoke still hanging over the battle-field, its light shall fall with equal radiance on the blue and the gray.

The Burial of the Guns

[THOMAS NELSON PAGE]

Lee surrendered the remnant of his army at Appomattox, April 9, 1865, and yet a couple of days later the old Colonel's battery lay intrenched right in the mountain-pass where it had halted three days before. Two weeks previously it had been detailed with a light division sent to meet and repel a force which it was understood was coming in by way of the southwest valley to strike Lee in the rear of his long line from Richmond to Petersburg. It had done its work. The mountain-pass had been seized and held, and the Federal force had not gotten by that road within the blue rampart which guarded on that side the heart of Virginia. This pass, which was the key to the main line of passage over the mountains, had been assigned by the commander of the division to the old Colonel and his old battery, and they had held it. The position taken by the battery had been chosen with a soldier's eye. A better place could not have been selected to hold the pass. It was its highest point, just where the road crawled over the shoulder of the mountain along the limestone cliff, a hundred feet sheer above the deep river, where its waters had cut their way in ages past, and now lay deep and silent, as if resting after their arduous toil before they began to boil over the great bowlders which filled the bed a hundred or more yards below.

The little plateau at the top guarded the descending road on either side for nearly a mile, and the mountain on the other side of the river was the centre of a clump of rocky, heavily timbered spurs, so inaccessible that no feet but those of wild animals or of the hardiest hunter had ever climbed it. On the side of the river on which the road lay, the only path out over the mountain except the road itself was a charcoal-burner's track, dwindling at times to a footway known only to the mountain-folk, which a picket at the top could hold against an army. The position, well defended, was impregnable, and it was well defended. This the general of the division knew when he detailed the old Colonel and gave him his order to hold the pass until relieved, and not let his guns fall into the hands of the enemy. He knew both the Colonel and his battery. The battery was one of the oldest in the army. It had been in the service since April, 1861, and its commander had come to be known as "The Wheel Horse of his division." He was, perhaps, the oldest officer of his rank in his branch of the service. Although he had bitterly opposed secession, and was many years past the age of service when the war came on, yet as soon as the President called on the State for her quota of troops to coerce South Carolina, he had raised and uniformed an artillery company, and offered it, not to the President of the United States, but to the Governor of Virginia.

It is just at this point that he suddenly looms up to me as a soldier; the relation he never wholly lost to me afterward, though I knew him for many, many years of peace. His gray coat with the red facing and the bars on the collar; his military cap; his gray flannel shirt—it was the first time I ever saw him wear anything but immaculate linen—his high boots; his horse caparisoned with a black, high-peaked saddle, with crupper and breast-girth, instead of the light English hunting-saddle to which I had been accustomed, all come before me now as if it were but the other day. I remember but little beyond it, yet I remember, as if it were yesterday, his leaving home, and the scenes which immediately preceded it; the excitement created by the news of the President's call for troops; the unanimous judgment that it meant war; the immediate determination of the old Colonel, who had hitherto opposed secession, that it must be met; the suppressed agitation on the plantation, attendant upon the tender of his services and the Governor's acceptance of them. The prompt and continuous work incident to the enlistment of the men, the bustle of preparation, and all the scenes of that time, come before me now. It turned the calm current of the life of an old and placid country neighborhood, far from any city or centre, and stirred it into a boiling torrent, strong enough, or fierce enough to cut its way and join the general torrent which was bearing down and sweeping everything before it. It seemed but a minute before the quiet old plantation, in which the harvest, the corn-shucking, and the Christmas holidays alone marked the passage of the quiet seasons, and where a strange carriage or a single horseman coming down the big road was an event in life, was turned into a depot of war-supplies, and the neighborhood became a parade-ground. The old Colonel, not a colonel yet, nor even a captain, except by brevet, was on his horse by day-break and off on his rounds through the plantations and the pines enlisting his company. The office in the yard, heretofore one in name only, became one now in reality, and a table was set out piled with papers, pens, ink, books of tactics and regulation, at which men were accepted and enrolled. Soldiers seemed to spring from the ground, as they did from the sowing of the dragon's teeth in the days of Cadmus. Men came up the high road or down the paths across the fields, sometimes singly, but oftener in little parties of two or three, and, asking for the Captain, entered the office as private citizens and came out soldiers enlisted for the war. There was nothing heard of on the plantation except fighting; white and black, all were at work, and all were eager; the servants contended for the honor of going with their master; the women flocked to the house to assist in the work of preparation, cutting out and making under-clothes, knitting socks, picking lint, preparing bandages, and sewing on uniforms; for many of the men who had enlisted were of the poorest class, far too poor to furnish anything themselves, and their equipment had to be contributed mainly by wealthier neighbors. The work was carried on at night as well as by day, for the occasion was urgent. Meantime the men were being drilled by the Captain and his lieutenants, who had been militia officers of old. We were carried to see the drill at the cross-roads, and a brave sight it seemed to us: the lines marching and countermarching in the field, with the horses galloping as they wheeled amid clouds of dust, at the hoarse commands of the excited officers, and the roadside lined with spectators of every age and condition. I recall the arrival of the messenger one night, with the telegraphic order to the Captain to report with his company at "Camp Lee" immediately; the hush in the parlor that attended its reading; then the forced beginning of the conversation afterwards in a somewhat strained and unnatural key, and the Captain's quick and decisive outlining of his plans.

Within the hour a dozen messengers were on their way in various directions to notify the members of the command of the summons, and to deliver the order for their attendance at a given point next day. It seemed that a sudden and great change had come. It was the actual appearance of what had hitherto only been theoretical—war. The next morning the Captain, in full uniform, took leave of the assembled plantation, with a few solemn words commending all he left behind to God, and galloped away up the big road to join and lead his battery to the war, and to be gone just four years.

Within a month he was on "the Peninsula" with Magruder, guarding Virginia on the east against the first attack. His camp was first at Yorktown and then on Jamestown Island, the honor having been assigned his battery of guarding the oldest cradle of the race on this continent. It was at "Little Bethel" that his guns were first trained on the enemy, and that the battery first saw what they had to do, and from this time until the middle of April, 1865, they were in service, and no battery saw more service or suffered more in it. Its story was a part of the story of the Southern Army in Virginia. The Captain was a rigid disciplinarian, and his company had more work to do than most new companies. A pious churchman, of the old puritanical type not uncommon to

Virginia, he looked after the spiritual as well as the physical welfare of his men, and his chaplain or he read prayers at the head of his company every morning during the war. At first he was not popular with the men, he made the duties of camp life so onerous to them, it was "nothing but drilling and praying all the time," they said. But he had not commanded very long before they came to know the stuff that was in him. He had not been in service a year before he had had four horses shot under him, and when later on he was offered the command of a battalion, the old company petitioned to be one of his batteries, and still remained under his command. Before the first year was out the battery had, through its own elements, and the discipline of the Captain, become a cohesive force, and a distinct integer in the Army of Northern Virginia. Young farmer recruits knew of its prestige and expressed preference for it of many batteries of rapidly growing or grown reputation. Owing to its high stand, the old and clumsy guns with which it had started out were taken from it, and in their place was presented a battery of four fine, brass, twelve-pound Napoleons of the newest and most approved kind, and two three-inch Parrotts, all captured. The men were as pleased with them as children with new toys. The care and attention needed to keep them in prime order broke the monotony of camp life. They soon had abundant opportunities to test their power. They worked admirably, carried far, and were extraordinarily accurate in their aim. The men from admiration of their guns grew to have first a pride in, and then an affection for, them, and gave them nicknames as they did their comrades; the four Napoleons being dubbed "The Evangelists," and the two rifles being "The Eagle," because of its scream and force, and "The Cat," because when it became hot from rapid firing "It jumped," they said, "like a cat." From many a hill-top in Virginia, Maryland, and Pennsylvania "The Evangelists" spoke their hoarse message of battle and death, "The Eagle" screamed her terrible note, and "The Cat" jumped as she spat her deadly shot from her hot throat. In the Valley of Virginia; on the levels of Henrico and Hanover; on the slopes of Manassas; in the woods of Chancellorsville; on the heights of Fredericksburg; at Antietam and Gettysburg; in the Spottsylvania wilderness, and again on the Hanover levels and on the lines before Petersburg, the old guns through nearly four years roared from fiery throats their deadly messages. The history of the battery was bound up with the history of Lee's army. A rivalry sprang up among the detachments of the different guns, and their several records were jealously kept. The number of duels each gun was in was carefully counted, every scar got in battle was treasured, and the men around their camp-fires, at their scanty messes, or on the march, bragged of them among themselves and avouched them as witnesses. New recruits coming in to fill the gaps made by the killed and disabled, readily fell in with the common mood and caught the spirit like a contagion. It was not an uncommon thing for a wheel to be smashed in by a shell, but if it happened to one gun oftener than to another there was envy. Two of the Evangelists seemed to be especially favored in this line, while the Cat was so exempt as to become the subject of some derision. The men stood by the guns till they were knocked to pieces, and when the fortune of the day went against them, had with their own hands oftener than once saved them after most of their horses were killed.

This had happened in turn to every gun, the men at times working like beavers in mud up to their thighs and under a murderous fire to get their guns out. Many a man had been killed tugging at trail or wheel when the day was against them; but not a gun had ever been lost. At last the evil day arrived. At Winchester a sudden and impetuous charge for a while swept everything before it, and carried the knoll where the old battery was posted; but all the guns were got out by the toiling and rapidly dropping men, except the Cat, which was captured with its entire detachment working at it until they were surrounded and knocked from the piece by cavalrymen. Most of the men who were not killed were retaken before the day was over, with many guns; but the Cat was lost. She remained in the enemy's hands and probably was being turned against her old comrades and lovers. The company was inconsolable. The death of comrades was too natural and common a thing to depress the men beyond what such occurrences necessarily did; but to lose a gun! It was like losing the old Colonel; it was worse: a gun was ranked as a brigadier; and the Cat was equal to a major-general. The other guns seemed lost without her; the Eagle especially, which generally went next to her, appeared to the men to have a lonely and subdued air. The battery was no longer the same: it seemed broken and depleted, shrunken to a mere section. It was worse than Cold Harbor, where over half the men were killed or wounded. The old Captain, now Colonel of the battalion, appreciated the loss and apprehended its effect on the men as much as they themselves did, and application was made for a gun to take the place of the lost piece; but there was none to be had, as the men said they had known all along. It was added—perhaps by a department clerk—that if they wanted a gun to take the place of the one they had lost, they had better capture it. "By ——, we will," they said—adding epithets, intended for the department clerk in his "bomb-proof," not to be printed in this record—and they did. For some time afterwards in every engagement into which they got there used to be speculation among them as to whether the Cat were not there on the other side; some of the men swearing they could tell her report, and even going to the rash length of offering bets on her presence.

By one of those curious coincidences, as strange as anything in fiction, a new general had, in 1864, come down across the Rapidan to take Richmond, and the old battery had found a hill-top in the line in which Lee's army lay stretched across "the Wilderness" country to stop him. The day, though early in May, was a hot one, and the old battery, like most others, had suffered fearfully. Two of the guns had had wheels cut down by shells and the men had been badly cut up; but the fortune of the day had been with Lee, and a little before nightfall, after a terrible fight, there was a rapid advance, Lee's infantry sweeping everything before it, and the artillery, after opening the way for the charge, pushing along with it; now unlimbering as some vantage-ground was gained, and using canister with deadly effect; now driving ahead again so rapidly that it was mixed up with the muskets when the long line of breastworks was carried with a rush, and a line of guns were caught still hot from their rapid work. As the old battery, with lathered horses and smoke-grimed men, swung up the crest and unlimbered on the captured breastwork, a cheer went up which was heard even above the long general yell of the advancing line, and for a moment half the men in the battery crowded together around some object on the edge of the redoubt, yelling like madmen. The next instant they divided, and there was the Cat, smoke-grimed and blood-stained and still sweating hot from her last fire, being dragged from her muddy ditch by as many men as could get hold of trail-rope or wheel, and rushed into her old place beside the Eagle, in time to be double-shotted with canister to the muzzle, and to pour it from among her old comrades into her now retiring former masters. Still, she had a new carriage, and her record was lost, while those of the other guns had been faithfully kept by the men. This made a difference in her position for which even the bullets in her wheels did not wholly atone; even Harris, the sergeant of her detachment, felt that.

It was only a few days later, however, that abundant atonement was made. The new general did not retire across the Rapidan after his first defeat, and a new battle had to be fought: a battle, if anything, more furious, more terrible than the first, when the dead filled the trenches and covered the fields. He simply marched by the left flank, and Lee marching by the right flank to head him, flung himself upon him again at Spottsylvania Court-House. That day the Cat, standing in her place behind the new and temporary breastwork thrown up when the battery was posted, had the felloes of her wheels, which showed above the top of the bank, entirely cut away by Minie-bullets, so that when she jumped in the recoil her wheels smashed and let her down. This covered all old scores. The other guns had been cut down by shells or solid shot; but never before had one been gnawed down by musket-balls. From this time all through the campaign the Cat held her own beside her brazen and bloody sisters, and in the cold trenches before Petersburg that winter, when the new general—Starvation—had joined the one already there, she made her bloody mark as often as any gun on the long lines.

Thus the old battery had come to be known, as its old commander, now colonel of a battalion, had come to be known by those in yet higher command. And when in the opening spring of 1865 it became apparent to the leaders of both armies that the long line could not longer be held if a force should enter behind it, and, sweeping the one partially unswept portion of Virginia, cut the railways in the southwest, and a man was wanted to command the artillery in the expedition sent to meet this force, it was not remarkable that the old Colonel and his battalion should be selected for the work. The force sent out was but small; for the long line was worn to a thin one in those days, and great changes were taking place, the consequences of which were known only to the commanders. In a few days the commander of the expedition found that he must divide his small force for a time, at least, to accomplish his purpose, and sending the old Colonel with one battery of artillery to guard one pass, must push on over

the mountain by another way to meet the expected
force, if possible, and repel it before it crossed the farther range. Thus the old battery, on an April evening
of 1865, found itself toiling alone up the steep
mountain road which leads above the river to the
gap, which formed the chief pass in that part of the
Blue Ridge. Both men and horses looked, in the dim
and waning light of the gray April day, rather like
shadows of the beings they represented than the
actual beings themselves. And anyone seeing them as
they toiled painfully up, the thin horses floundering
in the mud, and the men, often up to their knees,
tugging at the sinking wheels, now stopping to rest,
and always moving so slowly that they seemed
scarcely to advance at all, might have thought them
the ghosts of some old battery lost from some long
gone and forgotten war on that deep and desolate
mountain road. Often, when they stopped, the
blowing of the horses and the murmuring of the
river in its bed below were the only sounds heard,
and the tired voices of the men when they spoke
among themselves seemed hardly more articulate
sounds than they. Then the voice of the mounted
figure on the roan horse half hidden in the mist
would cut in, clear and inspiring, in a tone of
encouragement more than of command, and everything would wake up: the drivers would shout and
crack their whips; the horses would bend themselves
on the collars and flounder in the mud; the men

would spring once more to the mud-clogged wheels, and the slow ascent would begin again.

The orders to the Colonel, as has been said, were brief: To hold the pass until he received further instructions, and not to lose his guns. To be ordered, with him, was to obey. The last streak of twilight brought them to the top of the pass; his soldier's instinct and a brief recognizance made earlier in the day told him that this was his place, and before day-break next morning the point was as well fortified as a night's work by weary and supperless men could make it. A prettier spot could not have been found for the purpose; a small plateau, something over an acre in extent, where a charcoal-burner's hut had once stood, lay right at the top of the pass. It was a little higher on either side than in the middle, where a small brook, along which the charcoal-burner's track was yet visible, came down from the wooded mountain above, thus giving a natural crest to aid the fortification on either side, with open space for the guns, while the edge of the wood coming down from the mountain afforded shelter for the camp.

As the battery was unsupported it had to rely on itself for everything, a condition which most sol-diers by this time were accustomed to. A dozen or so of rifles were in the camp, and with these pickets were armed and posted. The pass had been seized none too soon; a scout brought in the information before nightfall that the invading force had crossed the farther range before that sent to meet it could get there, and taking the nearest road had avoided the main body opposing it, and been met only by a rapidly moving detachment, nothing more than a scouting party, and now were advancing rapidly on the road on which they were posted, evidently meaning to seize the pass and cross the mountain at this point. The day was Sunday; a beautiful Spring Sunday; but it was no Sabbath for the old battery. All day the men worked, making and strengthening their redoubt to guard the pass, and by the next morning, with the old battery at the top, it was impregnable. They were just in time. Before noon their vedettes brought in word that the enemy were ascending the mountain, and the sun had hardly turned when the advance guard rode up, came within range of the picket, and were fired on.

It was apparent that they supposed the force there only a small one, for they retired and soon came up again reinforced in some numbers, and a sharp little skirmish ensued, hot enough to make them more prudent afterwards, though the picket retired up the mountain. This gave them encouragement and probably misled them, for they now advanced boldly. They saw the redoubt on the crest as they came on, and unlimbering a section or two, flung a few shells up at it, which either fell short or passed over without doing material damage. None of the guns was allowed to respond, as the distance was too great

with the ammunition the battery had, and, indiffer-
ent as it was, it was too precious to be wasted in a
duel at an ineffectual range. Doubtless deceived by
this, the enemy came on in force, being obliged by
the character of the ground to keep almost entirely
to the road, which really made them advance in column. The battery waited. Under orders of the
Colonel the guns standing in line were double-
shotted with canister, and, loaded to the muzzle,
were trained down to sweep the road at from four to
five hundred yards' distance. And when the column
reached this point the six guns, aimed by old and
skilful gunners, at a given word swept road and
mountain-side with a storm of leaden hail. It was a
fire no mortal man could stand up against, and the
practised gunners rammed their pieces full again, and
before the smoke had cleared or the reverberation
had died away among the mountains, had fired the
guns again and yet again. The road was cleared of
living things when the draught setting down the
river drew the smoke away; but it was no discredit to
the other force; for no army that was ever uniformed
could stand against that battery in that pass. Again
and again the attempt was made to get a body of
men up under cover of the woods and rocks on the
mountain-side, while the guns below utilized their
better ammunition from longer range; but it was
useless. Although one of the lieutenants and several
men were killed in the skirmish, and a number more

were wounded, though not severely, the old battery commanded the mountain-side, and its skilful gunners swept it at every point the foot of man could scale. The sun went down flinging his last flame on a victorious battery still crowning the mountain pass. The dead were buried by night in a corner of the little plateau, borne to their last bivouac on the old gun-carriages which they had stood by so often—which the men said would "sort of ease their minds."

The next day the fight was renewed, and with the same result. The old battery in its position was unconquerable. Only one fear now faced them; their ammunition was getting as low as their rations; another such day or half-day would exhaust it. A sergeant was sent back down the mountain to try to get more, or, if not, to get tidings. The next day it was supposed the fight would be renewed; and the men waited, alert, eager, vigilant, their spirits high, their appetite for victory whetted by success. The men were at their breakfast, or what went for breakfast, scanty at all times, now doubly so, hardly deserving the title of a meal, so poor and small were the portions of cornmeal, cooked in their frying-pans, which went for their rations, when the sound of artillery below broke on the quiet air. They were on their feet in an instant and at the guns, crowding upon the breastwork to look or to listen; for the road, as far as could be seen down the mountain, was empty except for their own picket, and lay as quiet as if sleeping in the balmy air. And yet volley after volley of artillery came rolling up the mountain. What could it mean? That the rest of their force had come up and was engaged with that at the foot of the mountain? The Colonel decided to be ready to go and help them; to fall on the enemy in the rear; perhaps they might capture the entire force. It seemed the natural thing to do, and the guns were limbered up in an incredibly short time, and a roadway made through the intrenchment, the men working like beavers under the excitement. Before they had left the redoubt, however, the vedettes sent out returned and reported that there was no engagement going on, and the firing below seemed to be only practising. There was quite a stir in the camp below; but they had not even broken camp. This was mysterious. Perhaps it meant that they had received reinforcements, but it was a queer way of showing it. The old Colonel sighed as he thought of the good ammunition they could throw away down there, and of his empty limber-chests. It was necessary to be on the alert, however; the guns were run back into their old places, and the horses picketed once more back among the trees. Meantime he sent another messenger back, this time a courier, for he had but one commissioned officer left, and the picket below was strengthened.

The morning passed and no one came; the day wore on and still no advance was made by the force below. It was suggested that the enemy had left; he had, at least, gotten enough of that battery. A reconnaissance, however, showed that he was still encamped at the foot of the mountain. It was conjectured that he was trying to find a way around to take them in the rear, or to cross the ridge by the footpath. Preparation was made to guard more closely the mountain-path across the spur, and a detachment was sent up to strengthen the picket there. The waiting told on the men and they grew bored and restless. They gathered about the guns in groups and talked; talked of each piece some, but not with the old spirit and vim; the loneliness of the mountain seemed to oppress them; the mountains stretching up so brown and gray on one side of them, and so brown and gray on the other, with their bare, dark forests soughing from time to time as the wind swept up the pass. The minds of the men seemed to go back to the time when they were not so alone, but were part of a great and busy army, and some of them fell to talking of the past, and the battles they had figured in, and of the comrades they had lost. They told them off in a slow and colorless way, as if it were all part of the past as much as the dead they named. One hundred and nineteen times they had been in action. Only seventeen men were left of the eighty odd who had first enlisted in the battery, and of these four were at home crippled for life. Two of the oldest men had been among the half-dozen who had fallen in the skirmish just the day before. It looked tolerably hard to be killed that way after passing for four years through such battles as they had been in; and both had wives and children at home, too, and not a cent to leave them to their names. They agreed calmly that they'd have to "sort of look after them a little" if they ever got home. These were some of the things they talked about as they pulled their old worn coats about them, stuffed their thin, weather-stained hands in their ragged pockets to warm them, and squatted down under the breastwork to keep a little out of the wind. One thing they talked about a good deal was something to eat. They described meals they had had at one time or another as personal adventures, and discussed the chances of securing others in the future as if they were prizes of fortune. One listening and seeing their thin, worn faces and their wasted frames might have supposed they were starving, and they were, but they did not say so.

Towards the middle of the afternoon there was a sudden excitement in the camp. A dozen men saw them at the same time: a squad of three men down the road at the farthest turn, past their picket; but an advancing column could not have created as much excitement, for the middle man carried a white flag. In a minute every man in the battery was on the breastwork. What could it mean! It was a long way off, nearly half a mile, and the flag was small: possibly only a pocket-handkerchief or a napkin; but it was held aloft as a flag unmistakably. A hundred conjectures were indulged in. Was it a summons to surrender? A request for an armistice for some purpose? Or was it a trick to ascertain their number and position? Some held one view, some another. Some extreme ones thought a shot ought to be fired over them to warn them not to come on; no flags of truce were wanted. The old Colonel, who had walked to the edge of the plateau outside the redoubt and taken his position where he could study the advancing figures with his field-glass, had not spoken. The lieutenant who was next in command to him had walked out after him, and stood near him, from time to time dropping a word or two of conjecture in a half-audible tone; but the Colonel had not answered a word; perhaps none was expected. Suddenly he took his glass down, and gave an order to the lieutenant: "Take two men and meet them at the turn yonder; learn their business; and act as your best judgment advises. If necessary to bring the messenger farther, bring only the officer who has the flag, and halt him at that rock yonder, where I will join him." The tone was as placid as if such an occurrence came every day. Two minutes later the lieutenant was on his way down the mountain and the Colonel had the men in ranks. His face was as grave and his manner as quiet as usual, neither more nor less so. The men were in a state of suppressed excitement. Having put them in charge of the second sergeant the Colonel returned to the breastwork. The two officers were slowly ascending the hill, side by side, the bearer of the flag, now easily distinguishable in his jaunty uniform as a captain of cavalry, talking, and the lieutenant in faded gray, faced with yet more faded red, walking beside him with a face white even at that distance, and lips shut as though they would never open again. They halted at the big bowlder which the Colonel had indicated, and the lieutenant, having saluted ceremoniously, turned to come up to the camp; the Colonel, however, went down to meet him. The two men met, but there was no spoken question; if the Colonel inquired it was only with the eyes. The lieutenant spoke, however. "He says," he began and stopped, then began again—"he says, General Lee—" again he choked, then blurted out, "I believe it is all a lie—a damned lie."

"Not dead? Not killed?" said the Colonel, quickly.

"No, not so bad as that; surrendered: surrendered his entire army at Appomattox day before yesterday. I believe it is all a damned lie," he broke out again, as if the hot denial relieved him. The Colonel simply turned away his face and stepped a pace or two off, and the two men stood motionless back to back for more than a minute. Then the Colonel stirred.

"Shall I go back with you?" the lieutenant asked, huskily.

The Colonel did not answer immediately. Then he said: "No, go back to camp and await my return." He said nothing about not speaking of the report. He knew it was not needed. Then he went down the hill slowly alone, while the lieutenant went up to the camp.

The interview between the two officers beside the bowlder was not a long one. It consisted of a brief statement by the Federal envoy of the fact of Lee's surrender two days before near Appomattox Court-House, with the sources of his information, coupled with a formal demand on the Colonel for his surrender. To this the Colonel replied that he had been detached and put under command of another officer for a specific purpose, and that his orders were to hold that pass, which he should do until he was instructed otherwise by his superior in command. With that they parted, ceremoniously, the Federal captain returning to where he had left his horse in charge of his companions a little below, and the old Colonel coming slowly up the hill to camp. The men were at once set to work to meet any attack which might be made. They knew that the message was of grave import, but not of how grave. They thought it meant that another attack would be made immediately, and they sprang to their work with renewed vigor, and a zeal as fresh as if it were but the beginning and not the end.

The time wore on, however, and there was no demonstration below, though hour after hour it was expected and even hoped for. Just as the sun sank into a bed of blue cloud a horseman was seen coming up the darkened mountain from the eastward side, and in a little while practised eyes reported him one of their own men—the sergeant who had been sent back the day before for ammunition. He was alone, and had something white before him on his horse—it could not be the ammunition; but perhaps that might be coming on behind. Every step of his jaded horse was anxiously watched. As he drew near, the lieutenant, after a word with the Colonel, walked down to meet him, and there was a short colloquy in the muddy road; then they came back together and slowly entered the camp, the sergeant handing down a bag of corn which he had got somewhere below, with the grim remark to his comrades, "There's your rations," and going at once to the Colonel's camp-fire, a little to one side among the trees, where the Colonel awaited him. A long conference was held, and then the sergeant left to take his luck with his mess, who were already parching the corn he had brought for their supper, while the lieutenant made the round of the camp; leaving the Colonel seated alone on a log by his camp-fire. He sat without moving, hardly stirring until the lieutenant returned from his round. A minute later the men were called from the guns and made to fall into line. They were silent, tremulous with suppressed excitement; the most sun-burned and weather-stained of them a little pale; the meanest, raggedest, and most insignificant not unimpressive in the deep and solemn silence with which they stood, their eyes fastened on the Colonel, waiting for him to speak. He stepped out in front of them, slowly ran his eye along the irregular line, up and down, taking in every man in his glance, resting on some longer than on others, the older men, then dropped them to the ground, and then suddenly, as if with an effort, began to speak. His voice had a somewhat metallic sound, as if it were restrained; but it was otherwise the ordinary tone of command. It was not much that he said: simply that it had become his duty to acquaint them with the information which he had received: that General Lee had surrendered two days before at Appomattox Court-House, yielding to overwhelming numbers; that this afternoon when he had first heard the report he had questioned its truth, but that it had been confirmed by one of their own men, and no longer admitted of doubt; that the rest of their own force, it was learned, had been captured, or had disbanded, and the enemy was now on both sides of the mountain; that a demand had been made on him that morning to surrender too; but that he had orders which he felt held good until they were countermanded, and he had declined. Later intelligence satisfied him that to attempt to hold out further would be useless, and would involve needless waste of life; he had determined, therefore, not to attempt to hold their position longer; but to lead them out, if possible, so as to avoid being made prisoners and enable them to reach home sooner and aid their families. His orders were not to let his guns fall into the enemy's hands, and he should take the only step possible to prevent it. In fifty minutes he should call the battery into line once more, and roll the guns over the cliff into the river, and immediately afterwards, leaving the wagons there, he would try to lead them across the mountain, and as far as they could go in a body without being liable to capture, and then he should disband them, and his responsibility for them would end. As it was necessary to make some preparations he would now dismiss them to prepare any rations they might have and get ready to march.

All this was in the formal manner of a common order of the day; and the old Colonel had spoken in measured sentences, with little feeling in his voice. Not a man in the line had uttered a word after the first sound, half exclamation, half groan, which had burst from them at the announcement of Lee's surrender. After that they had stood in their tracks like rooted trees, as motionless as those on the mountain behind them, their eyes fixed on their commander, and only the quick heaving up and down the dark line, as of horses over-laboring, told of the emotion which was shaking them. The Colonel, as he ended, half-turned to his subordinate officer at the end of the dim line, as though he were about to turn the company over to him to be dismissed; then faced the line again, and taking a step nearer, with a sudden movement of his hands towards the men as though he would have stretched them out to them, began again:

"Men," he said, and his voice changed at the word, and sounded like a father's or a brother's, "My men, I cannot let you go so. We were neighbors when the war began—many of us, and some not here to-night; we have been more since then—comrades, brothers in arms; we have all stood for one thing—for Virginia and the South; we have all done our duty—tried to do our duty; we have fought a good fight, and now it seems to be over, and we have been overwhelmed by numbers, not whipped—and we are going home. We have the future before us— we don't know just what it will bring, but we can stand a good deal. We have proved it. Upon us depends the South in the future as in the past. You have done your duty in the past, you will not fail in the future. Go home and be honest, brave, self-sacrificing, God-fearing citizens, as you have been soldiers, and you need not fear for Virginia and the South. The war may be over; but you will ever be ready to serve your country. The end may not be as we wanted it, prayed for it, fought for it; but we can trust God; the end in the end will be the best that could be; even if the South is not free she will be better and stronger that she fought as she did. Go home and bring up your children to love her, and though you may have nothing else to leave them, you can leave them the heritage that they are sons of men who were in Lee's army."

He stopped, looked up and down the ranks again, which had instinctively crowded together and drawn around him in a half-circle; made a sign to the lieutenant to take charge, and turned abruptly on his heel to walk away. But as he did so, the long pent-up emotion burst forth. With a wild cheer the men seized him, crowding around and hugging him, as with protestations, prayers, sobs, oaths—broken, incoherent, inarticulate—they swore to be faithful, to live loyal forever to the South, to him, to Lee. Many of them cried like children; others offered to go down and have one more battle on the plain. The old Colonel soothed them, and quieted their excitement, and then gave a command about the preparations to be made. This called them to order at once; and in a few minutes the camp was as orderly and quiet as usual: the fires were replenished; the scanty stores were being overhauled; the place was selected, and being got ready to roll the guns over the cliff; the camp was being ransacked for such articles as could be carried, and all preparations were being hastily made for their march.

The old Colonel having completed his arrangements sat down by his camp-fire with paper and pencil, and began to write; and as the men finished their work they gathered about in groups, at first around their camp-fires, but shortly strolled over to where the guns still stood at the breastwork, black and vague in the darkness. Soon they were all assembled about the guns. One after another they visited, closing around it and handling it from muzzle to trail as a man might a horse to try its sinew and bone, or a child to feel its fineness and warmth. They were for the most part silent, and when any sound came through the dusk from them to the officers at their fire, it was murmurous and fitful as of men speaking low and brokenly. There was no sound of the noisy controversy which was generally heard, the give-and-take of the camp-fire, the firing backwards and forwards that went on on the march; if a compliment was paid a gun by one of its special detachment, it was accepted by the others; in fact, those who had generally run it down now seemed most anxious to accord the piece praise. Presently a small number of the men returned to a camp-fire, and, building it up, seated themselves about it, gathering closer and closer together until they were in a little knot. One of them appeared to be writing, while two or three took up flaming chunks from the fire and held them as torches for him to see by. In time the entire company assembled about them, standing in respectful silence, broken only occasionally by a reply from one or another to some question from the scribe. After a little there was a sound of a roll-call, and reading and a short colloquy followed, and then two men, one with a paper in his hand, approached the fire beside which the officers sat still engaged.

"What is it, Harris?" said the Colonel to the man with the paper, who bore remnants of the chevrons of a sergeant on his stained and faded jacket.

"If you please, sir," he said, with a salute, "we have been talking it over, and we'd like this paper to go in along with that you're writing." He held it out to the lieutenant, who was the nearer and had reached forward to take it. "We s'pose you're agoin' to bury it with the guns," he said, hesitatingly, as he handed it over.

"What is it?" asked the Colonel, shading his eyes with his hands.

"It's just a little list we made out in and among us," he said, "with a few things we'd like to put in, so's if anyone ever hauls 'em out they'll find it there to tell what the old battery was, and if they don't, it'll be in one of 'em down thar 'til judgment, an' it'll sort of ease our minds a bit." He stopped and waited as a man who had delivered his message. The old Colonel had risen and taken the paper, and now held it with a firm grasp, as if it might blow away with the rising wind. He did not say a word, but his hand shook a little as he proceeded to fold it carefully, and there was a burning gleam in his deep-set eyes, back under his bushy, gray brows.

"Will you sort of look over it, sir, if you think it's worth while? We was in a sort of hurry and we had to put it down just as we come to it; we didn't have time to pick our ammunition; and it ain't written the best in the world, nohow." He waited again, and the Colonel opened the paper and glanced down at it mechanically. It contained first a roster, headed by the list of six guns, named by name: "Matthew," "Mark," "Luke," and "John," "The Eagle," and "The Cat"; then of the men, beginning with the heading: "Those killed."

Then had followed "Those wounded," but this was marked out. Then came a roster of the company when it first entered service; then of those who had joined afterward; then of those who were present now. At the end of all there was this statement, not very well written, nor wholly accurately spelt:

"To Whom it may Concern: We, the above members of the old battery known, etc., of six guns, named, etc., commanded by the said Col. etc., left on the 11th day of April, 1865, have made out this roll of the battery, them as is gone and them as is left, to bury with the guns which the same we bury this night. We're all volunteers, every man; we joined the army at the beginning of the war, and we've stuck through to the end; sometimes we aint had much to eat, and sometimes we aint had nothin', but we've fought the best we could 119 battles and skirmishes as near as we can make out in four years, and never

lost a gun. Now we're agoin' home. We aint surrendered; just disbanded, and we pledges ourselves to
teach our children to love the South and General
Lee; and to come when we're called anywheres an'
anytime, so help us God."

There was a dead silence whilst the Colonel read.

"'Taint entirely accurite, sir, in one particular,"
said the sergeant, apologetically; "but we thought it
would be playin' it sort o' low down on the Cat if we
was to say we lost her unless we could tell about git-
tin' of her back, and the way she done since, and we
didn't have time to do all that." He looked around as
if to receive the corroboration of the other men,
which they signified by nods and shuffling.

The Colonel said it was all right, and the paper
should go into the guns.

"If you please, sir, the guns are all loaded," said the
sergeant; "in and about our last charge, too; and we'd
like to fire 'em off once more, jist for old times' sake
to remember 'em by, if you don't think no harm
could come of it?"

The Colonel reflected a moment and said it might
be done; they might fire each gun separately as they
rolled it over, or might get all ready and fire together,
and then roll them over, whichever they wished. This
was satisfactory.

The men were then ordered to prepare to march
immediately, and withdrew for the purpose. The
pickets were called in. In a short time they were ready,

horses and all, just as they would have been to march ordinarily, except that the wagons and caissons were packed over in one corner by the camp with the harness hung on poles beside them, and the guns stood in their old places at the breastwork ready to defend the pass. The embers of the sinking camp-fires threw a faint light on them standing so still and silent. The old Colonel took his place, and at a command from him in a somewhat low voice, the men, except a detail left to hold the horses, moved into company-front facing the guns. Not a word was spoken, except the words of command. At the order each detachment went to its gun; the guns were run back and the men with their own hands ran them up on the edge of the perpendicular bluff above the river, where, sheer below, its waters washed its base, as if to face an enemy on the black mountain the other side. The pieces stood ranged in the order in which they had so often stood in battle, and the gray, thin fog rising slowly and silently from the river deep down between the cliffs, and wreathing the mountain-side above, might have been the smoke from some unearthly battle fought in the dim pass by ghostly guns, yet posted there in the darkness, manned by phantom gunners, while phantom horses stood behind, lit vaguely up by phantom camp-fires. At the given word the laniards were pulled together, and together as one the six black guns, belching flame and lead, roared their last challenge on the misty night, sending a deadly hail of shot and shell, tearing the trees and splintering the rocks of the farther side, and sending the thunder reverberating through the pass and down the mountain, startling from its slumber the sleeping camp on the hills below, and driving the browsing deer and the prowling mountain-fox in terror up the mountain.

There was silence among the men about the guns for one brief instant and then such a cheer burst forth as had never broken from them even in battle: cheer on cheer, the long, wild, old familiar rebel yell for the guns they had fought with and loved.

The noise had not died away and the men behind were still trying to quiet the frightened horses when the sergeant, the same who had written, received from the hand of the Colonel a long package or roll which contained the records of the battery furnished by the men and by the Colonel himself, securely wrapped to make them water-tight, and it was rammed down the yet warm throat of the nearest gun: the Cat, and then the gun was tamped to the muzzle to make her water-tight, and, like her sisters, was spiked, and her vent tamped tight. All this took but a minute, and the next instant the guns were run up once more to the edge of the cliff; and the men stood by them with their hands still on them. A deadly silence fell on the men, and even the horses behind seemed to feel the spell. There was a long pause, in which not a breath was heard from any man, and the soughing of the tree-tops above and the rushing of the rapids below were the only sounds. They seemed to come from far, very far away. Then the Colonel said, quietly, "Let them go, and God be our helper, Amen." There was the noise in the darkness of trampling and scraping on the cliff-top for a second; the sound as of men straining hard together, and then with a pant it ceased all at once, and the men held their breath to hear. One second of utter silence; then one prolonged, deep, resounding splash sending up a great mass of white foam as the brass-pieces together plunged into the dark water below, and then the soughing of the trees and the murmur of the river came again with painful distinctness. It was full ten minutes before the Colonel spoke, though there were other sounds enough in the darkness, and some of the men, as the dark, outstretched bodies showed, were lying on the ground flat on their faces. Then the Colonel gave the command to fall in in the same quiet, grave tone he had used all night. The line fell in, the men getting to their horses and mounting in silence; the Colonel put himself at their head and gave the order of march, and the dark line turned in the darkness, crossed the little plateau between the smouldering camp-fires and the spectral caissons with the harness hanging beside them, and slowly entered the dim charcoal-burner's track. Not a word was spoken as they moved off. They might all have been phantoms. Only the sergeant in the rear, as he crossed the little breastwork which ran along the upper side and marked the boundary of the little camp, half turned and glanced at the dying fires, the low, newly made mounds in the corner, the abandoned caissons, and the empty redoubt, and said, slowly, in a low voice to himself, "Well, by God!"

A Woman's Wartime Journal
April 29, 1865

⟋⟍

[DOLLY SUMNER LUNT]

APRIL 29, 1865

B oys plowing in old house field. We are needing rain. Everything looks pleasant, but the
state of our country is very gloomy. General
Lee has surrendered to the victorious Grant. Well, if
it will only hasten the conclusion of this war, I am
satisfied. There has been something very strange in
the whole affair to me, and I can attribute it to nothing but the hand of Providence working out some
problem that has not yet been revealed to us poor
mortals. At the beginning of the struggle the minds
of men, their wills, their self-control, seemed to be
all taken from them in a passionate antagonism to
the coming-in President, Abraham Lincoln.

Our leaders, to whom the people looked for wisdom, led us into this, perhaps the greatest error of
the age. "We will not have this man to rule over us!"

was their cry. For years it has been stirring in the hearts of Southern politicians that the North was enriched and built up by Southern labor and wealth. Men's pockets were always appealed to and appealed to so constantly that an antagonism was excited which it has been impossible to allay. They did not believe that the North would fight. Said Robert Toombes: "I will drink every drop of blood they will shed." Oh, blinded men! Rivers deep and strong have been shed, and where are we now?—a ruined, subjugated people! What will be our future? is the question which now rests heavily upon the hearts of all.

This has been a month never to be forgotten. Two armies have surrendered. The President of the United States has been assassinated, Richmond evacuated, and Davis, President of the Confederacy, put to grief, to flight. The old flag has been raised again upon Sumter and an armistice accepted.

Sources

Excerpt from "Camp Jackson" by Winston Churchill from *The Crisis,* 1905.

"The Blue or the Gray" by John Fox, Jr. from *The Little Shepherd of Kingdom Come,* 1903.

"Bull Run" by Joseph A. Altsheler from *The Guns of Bull Run,* 1914.

"The Tedium of Camp" by John McElroy from *The Red Acorn,* 1883.

"What I Saw of Shiloh" by Ambrose Bierce, 1881.

"A Prisoner" by G. A. Henty from *With Lee in Virginia,* 1889.

"A Night" by Louisa May Alcott from *Hospital Sketches,* 1863.

"Vicksburg During the Trouble" by Mark Twain from *Life on the Mississippi*, 1883.

Excerpt from *My Cave Life in Vicksburg* by a Lady [Mary Ann Loughborough], 1864.

"The Fourteenth at Gettysburg" from *Harper's Weekly*, November 21, 1863.

"Completing My Disguise" by S. Emma E. Edmonds from *Nurse and Spy in the Union Army, Comprising the Adventures and Experiences of a Woman in Hospitals, Camps, and Battle-Fields*, 1865.

"The Charge in the Lane" by George Washington Cable from *The Cavalier*, 1901.

"Intensification of Suffering and Hatred" by Phoebe Yates Pember from *A Southern Woman's Story*, 1879.

"A Night Ride of the Wounded" by Randall Parrish from *My Lady of the North*, 1904.

Excerpt from "November 17–22, 1864" and "April 29, 1865" by Dolly Sumner Lunt from *A Woman's Wartime Journal: an Account of the Passage over a Georgia Plantation of Sherman's Army on the March to the Sea, as Recorded in the Diary of Dolly Sumner Lunt (Mrs. Thomas Burge)*, 1918.

"A Grey Sleeve" by Stephen Crane from *The Little Regiment, and Other Stories of the American Civil War*, 1896.

"A Horseman in the Sky" by Ambrose Bierce from
Tales of Soldiers and Civilians, 1891.

"The Last Shot" by Violetta from *Under Both Flags: A
Panorama of the Great Civil War,* 1896.

"The Burial of the Guns" by Thomas Nelson Page
from *The Burial of the Guns,* 1894.